LIBRARY
PACIFIC BIBLE INSTITUTE
2149 TUOLUMNE - FRESNO 21, CALIF.

*How to Preach the Word
With Variety*

How to Preach the Word With Variety

by
FRANK T. LITTORIN

BAKER BOOK HOUSE
Grand Rapids 6, Michigan
1953

Copyright, 1953, *by*
BAKER BOOK HOUSE

All rights in this book are reserved. No part may be reproduced in any manner without permission in writing from the publisher, except brief quotations used in connection with a review in a magazine or newspaper.

PRINTED IN THE UNITED STATES OF AMERICA

Foreword

In early December of 1923 a typical ordination service was held in the little Baptist Church in North Reading, Massachusetts. The platform was graced by visiting celebrities. Many friends had come for this important service, and the auditorium was crowded. This young pastor had the privilege of seeing a "full house," at least for this once. The usual banalities, frivolities and vitalities were said. Most of the details of what transpired that evening have long since been forgotten by that young pastor. Never has there ceased to ring in his ears one phrase of the "Charge to the Candidate," the phrase around which that "charge" was woven: "Preach the Word." How grateful I am to Nathan R. Wood, then President of Gordon College of Theology and Missions, who dinned that phrase into my ears that memorable night! What he said about it, I confess I do not know; but he said it and emphasized it effectively.

Though this challenge has scarcely ever ceased to resound, the challenge did not carry with it the inspiration and ability to perform. For several years I did not even seriously try to obey the command, though it often haunted me. The problem was, of course, "How?" Is it "preaching the Word" to dive off a convenient text (a pretext, is it not?) into the vortex of sermonic interpretation of life? Is a good starting point synonymous with a good start? Is a text for each sermon sufficient grounds for the claim to have fulfilled the apostolic injunction?

If men had been preaching the Word, we should not have so much "hobby horse riding" in the pulpit. The Word is keen, and keener than a two-edged sword, but it is also broad enough for the whole of man and all of humanity. If men had been preaching the Word, the Bible would not have lost its authority over the minds of the intellectual leaders of the world nor even with the blind beggars who would cry with Bartimaeus could they but sense Jesus of Nazareth passing by! We have let pseudo-scientists and -philosophers and -psychologists obscure the panacea in the Word, and Bartimaeus still sits begging "Have mercy on me!" but he does not know whom to address.

The Bible is authoritative in the field of religion, but it has largely lost its authority. This is true not only in the pew but in the pulpit to an heartbreaking degree. The preacher has become a dabbler in many things and is accepted as an authority in none. He may think his voice is that of authority, but the world, nor indeed his own church, will not regard him unless it please their fancy so to do. Had preachers been preaching the Word, this condition would not so largely obtain, at least not in reference to the preacher's authority within his own church! Furthermore, Christians are charged to give to any that ask a reason for the faith that is in them. But paltry few could explain the ground of their hope. Had we and our predecessors preached the Word, the pew would not be so lacking in this primary knowledge! The Bible is little used, known, or followed. The Bible is the least read bestseller in the world. The fault is in the pulpit, even before it is in the home, for preachers have not been preaching the Word!

All this is the merest shadowy introduction to what I have in mind. These problems were in mind for several years. Finally came the decision to "Preach the Word," but again, "How?" was a burning question. Volumes of sermons were read, and volumes on "homiletics" also. Some men did preach the Word. All advised it. Those who did were called "expositors," and almost all who advised preaching the Word referred to it as "Expository Preaching," but gave few specific instructions. And so "Expository Preaching" became the direct object of research. Again libraries were haunted and dusty volumes were searched, but largely in vain. Advice to preach the Word and examples of the finished work were found, but no "pointers to the path." In fact, to date, after having searched into literally hundreds of volumes only five volumes have been found that even pretend to give specific information on this which is so generally recognized as important matter.

Naturally then, one was driven to study sermons, in an attempt to discover by a laboratory study the methods used in producing them. Again, dust was disturbed as shelves were bared and sermons studied. These were studied not for content but for mechanics, not for color and line but for skeleton and framework. The works of Maclaren, Morgan and Meyer were the most valuable of all, and two volumes by John McNeill were helpful. But, even the study of sermons did not answer the problem. It was necessary to demonstrate explicitly each kind of machine, and the experimental field offered the most profit, with of course all that had been obtained by research as both goal and guide. We wanted to go where others had so profitably gone; but, as long as they had not blazed the trail, one must be blazed.

The first attempts were in the direction of the exegetical sermon. O the patience of Christians! How wonderfully people bore with me in those earlier "Expository" sermons, which now stand out as none other than exegetical studies brought into the pulpit. But people did stand these "Sermons" and asked for more. Continued reading and experimenting finally led to the writing down of what has been observed and discovered. This volume is the attempt so to describe the path that others may, if they will, experience the passionate pleasure in preaching the word that is the reward of the "Expositor."

This will not be — this cannot be — a conclusive and exhaustive volume on how to preach the Word. We have tried to make it clear. Ten years of teaching the subject to advanced students has served to demand very precise preparation, including constant experiment and review. However, in any homiletical work the real application of the principles contained therein is seen only in the personality and individuality of the preacher. We can suggest some principles of the art, but it is up to the artist to utilize them in his own way: in accord with his tools, his vision, and his canvas.

Contents

PART I. THE FUNDAMENTAL APPROACH

I. Preliminary Concepts 13

II. Basic Considerations 21

III. What Is Expository Preaching?
or Discovering a Definition 27

IV. The Exegetical-Expository Sermon 34
See Appendix I, page 127

PART II. APPLYING THE EXPOSITORY METHOD TO SELECTED COMPACT PORTIONS OF THE WORD

Introduction to Part II 46

I. The Microscopic Method 47
See Appendix II, page 129

II. The Paragraphing Method 51
See Appendix III, page 131

III. Spiritualizing 55
    A. Diverting 55
    See Appendix IV, page 132
    B. Illustrating 58
    See appendix V, page 134
    C. Portraiture as a Back-drop 60
    See Appendix VI, page 135

IV. Selecting the Desired Ideas 64
See Appendix VII, page 137

V. The Devotional Method 68
See Appendix VIII, page 138

VI. The Telescopic Approach 71
    See Appendix IX, page 139

PART III. APPLYING THE EXPOSITORY METHOD TO THE ENTIRE BIBLE IRRESPECTIVE OF ITS NATURAL DIVISIONS

Introduction to Part III 78
I. The Selective Method 79
    See Appendix X, page 142

II. Preaching from Biblical History 86
    See Appendix XI, page 143

III. Homiletically Interpreting Events 92
    See Appendix XII, page 146

IV. Preaching from Biblical Biographies 95
    See Appendix XIII, page 147

V. Sermons from Biographies Plus 100
    See Appendix XIV, page 149

VI. Sermon from Geography 104
    See Appendix XV, page 151

PART IV. PREACHING FROM VARIOUS KINDS OF BIBLICAL LITERATURE

Introduction to Part IV 110
I. Preaching on Parables 111
    See Appendix XVI, page 153

II. Preaching on Prayers 115
    See Appendix XVII, page 155

III. Preaching from the Psalms 118
    See Appendix XVIII, page 156

IV. Preaching from Prophetic and Apocalyptical Literature 121
Conclusion 123
Appendices 125

Part I

THE FUNDAMENTAL APPROACH

CHAPTER I

Preliminary Concepts

Before we turn to a study of method, or even consider evidences of need, there are certain preliminary and fundamental concepts which we must consider. These have to do with the value of expository preaching; they are calculated to lead us into this work if we have not thought it wise, or to strengthen our enthusiasm if we have tried it. They also affirm our ideal in regard to it and confirm our assertion of its value and need.

Our first concept is that *the Preacher must be a prophet*. Probably this is trite, but it is nonetheless true, and our attention is necessarily drawn to this idea. The Preacher who is merely a heckler or arouser, who deals with every topic under the sun except the Word of God will attract, and probably will attract crowds; but when he goes, so will the crowds go. Men will come to see what new thing or passing fancy is unearthed (or imagined) and will feed on it with gloating. But the lives of listeners may not be made beautiful or spiritual by this type of preaching. Most often they will not, though they accept the precepts presented. Fenelon (p. 174) quotes the epistle of Jerome to Napatian (ep. 34.), "When you shall preach to the church, seek neither to arouse the applause nor the groans of the people. . . . The sermon of the priest should be full of the Holy Scriptures. Do not be a mere declaimer, but a true teacher of the mysteries of God." We as preachers have a peculiar task, and when we speak as from the heart of God, men will listen. There is something about the cry of a prophet. Men may disobey, but they must listen.

It may not be remiss to remind ourselves that it is not necessary to "foretell" in order to be a prophet. In fact, this would be merely incidental as it was with the prophets of old. We must, as they, forthtell the message of God to the hearts of men. A. B. Davidson, in his book, *Old Testament Prophecy*, page 108, says, "The prophet took up the law and made it powerful, giving it flexibility and novelty of application." This, then, is our task. And unless the preacher is a prophet, he is merely an orator. He may be popular, even a "spell-binder," but as a preacher of the Gospel of Jesus Christ the Son of God, he fails unless he is also a prophet. He must speak the will, mind, purpose, desire, attitude, passion, of God into the sore and needy hearts of men. He must staunch the wounds of human hearts with divine panaceas, which alone are sufficient.

Another concept to which our attention is necessarily drawn is that *the preacher must use emotion*. Again, this may be trite, but it is true. The prophets of old were men of impassioned manner. They were not afraid utterly to lose themselves in their message. Too often we speak the Eternal Truths of God, giving His message to dying souls in a manner we use when we discuss the weather. However, we must not deceive ourselves. Tears that come from a mere psychological squeezing of the lachrymal ducts may mislead some souls, but soon our "play-acting" will be discovered and men will no longer heed our "emotional pleading." Surely also God sees through our deceit and will refuse to honor "crocodile tears." Dr. G. Campbell Morgan rightly says, "A man preaches well when his text masters him, not when he masters his text." The best and deepest emotion is that of a divine mastery in the soul of the preacher. Lips set on fire of God will set lives on fire in His behalf. Mere emotionalism is worthless. Cicero has well said, "Naught dries up sooner than a tear." And in another place he writes, "In great afflictions, weeping is a great relief. Thus, in a place of worship, in place of increasing tears only lessen the tension of emotion. Making people weep is a triumph (if it be one) as fleeting as it is easy." Yes, a preacher must use emotion, but it must be the emotion of a great mastery and a great passion, and not a clever imitation.

A third concept is that *the preacher must have a note of authority.* The "I'm from Missouri" attitude is not limited to natives of that state. Almost every statement in every realm is challenged by "Prove it." If the authority of the preacher comes from the assent of history or society or ethic or personality, always there will arise those with a contrary assertion or authority to lessen his effectiveness. Burdened and seeking hearts (and where are there other kinds?) are not so much concerned with "Thinkers in general conclude," as they are with "Thus saith the Lord." We need this authority and the fearlessness that goes with it. But, let a man's heart ache as he with authority denounces sin and warns of judgment on the sinner who fails to "repent and be converted." A man who can without a wrench in his bosom consign a sinner, however vile or blasphemous, to eternal perdition, is no follower of the prophets, nor surely of "The Prophet."

Authoritative preaching and prophetic preaching are one and the same. Prophetic preaching is not a matter of mechanics as such, nor even indeed of minute content. It is a matter of fire and passion and absolute domination by the Spirit of God in order that the will of God might be revealed to the people of God. Without a sure note of authority the preacher cannot deliver the message.

A fourth concept is that *the preacher must win his congregation to God.* Far too many congregations change complexions when the parsonage enfolds a new family. Too many pastors are expert at winning their people to themselves, and too few win them to a loyalty to God, regardless of the pastor. This is a fault that perhaps we cannot altogether correct, indeed perhaps eradication would not be altogether ideal. A certain amount of personal affection and loyalty is both beautiful and desirable as well as natural. But, to win men to God, the preacher must win them to the heart of God by direct appeal to their hearts with the message of God. How is one to do this? Passion and fire and authority all blend to this end. Goethe in "Faust" makes Faust, speaking to Wagner, his student, say,

"If feeling does not prompt, in vain you strive. If from the heart language does not come by its own impulse to impel the hearts of the hearers with communicated power, in vain you strive earnestly. Toil on forever; piece together fragments; cook up broken scraps of sentences, and blow with puffing breath a struggling light, glimmering confusedly now, now cold ashes; startle the school boys with your metaphors, and, if such food may suit your fancy, win the vain wonder of applauding children. But, never hope to stir the hearts of men and mould the many into one by words which come not native from the heart. . . ."

And, as he says later, "Be honest if you would be eloquent," and, "When you are in earnest, do you need to search for words?" The winning of the congregation must be heart-winning. Words of great men may come hot from many minds on many themes. The Word of God is that which must fire our hearts if we would thereby set aflame their hearts and "win the many into one by words which come native from the heart." This is, of course, closely akin to the thought of the preacher's need of emotion, in that it declares both the source and end of that emotion, as well as the means of imparting it to others.

Our fifth concept is that *the preacher must be an expositor* in order to succeed. Here we may strike our first opposition. However, thus far we do not mean that one must be what is ordinarily thought of as an "expository preacher" in order to succeed. We quote as illustration of our meaning, from *The Preacher and the King* (Bungener, p. 256, footnote), "A chapter in the Bible is not a block of marble to be carved . . . shall it be a god, a table or a basin? . . . The plan is all traced, the statue complete. It only remains to point out and animate it." As with "a chapter in the Bible," so also with the Will of God. In order to succeed in the holy ministry to which we by the Grace of God have been called, we must be "expositors," or, expound His plans and ideals and purposes. He has already "carved the statue." It is for us to "point out and animate" it. Surely in this sense we shall have full agreement in the statement that "one must be an expositor in order to succeed." Someone has said in this connection, "We are not heathen philosophers, finding out things. We are expositors of a revelation that settles things."

Preliminary Concepts

But, to go on, we dare to assert that in the exposition of the Book we can best obey this ideal. Further, we dare assert that exposition of the Book is our main task. We are overburdened with many secondary, and even extraneous duties, loaded upon our willing hands and enthusiastic minds by church and also by community. Yet we must not slight our main task. John Hall (Yale Lectures, 1875) says, "For remember that the great business of your life will be the exegesis of the Holy Word. To know, with the aid of grammar, dictionary, collation and exegesis of argument, what the Spirit of God intended to convey in a passage, is the first requirement of honest, faithful and effective preaching." We concur heartily that this is our main task.

Further, we assert that only in the faithful exposition of the Book shall we naturally and assuredly reach impartially all types of people in all walks of life. H. W. Beecher (Yale Lectures, 1872) says,

> "A much larger use should be made of expository preaching than is customary. It is an admirable way of familiarizing the people with the very text of the Scripture. There is an authority, which most audiences recognize, in the Word of God as delivered in the Sacred Scripture, which does not belong to ordinary teaching. Above all, the Bible is the best example of admirable mingling of fact, illustration, appeal, argument, poetry and emotion, not in their artificial forms, but conformable to nature. . . ."

And . . . "It will surprise one to see what wealth and diversity of topics will come up for illustration and discussion by means of expository preaching." Or, we might illustrate by quoting Bungener as he makes Abbe Fleury, one of the characters in *The Preacher and the King,* say (pp. 250-251), "It is one of the most beautiful prerogatives of the Bible, and, according to my opinion one of the strongest proofs of its divinity, that it furnishes to the most dissimilar minds an equally wholesome and nourishing food. I should say that the influence of the poets is like perfume which acts agreeably on the senses, while that of the Bible is like a perfume which penetrates every pore, and that the man thus impregnated transmits it naturally to all he touches." The doing then, of our main task, so far as material is concerned, will enable us to do our duty insofar as reaching all kinds of folks is concerned. Surely, a most worthy method of work for us to consider most carefully, and employ in the very best way discoverable!

We would go even deeper than this. We would assert that only in exposition, well prepared and presented, can one sound the very voice of God in the ears and hearts of the people before him. To emphasize this we quote from John Hall (Yale Lectures, 1875), who writes of the "wisdom of taking to a larger extent than we do, chapters or parts of chapters and expounding them." He says, "Let us be expository to a greater extent. Not that an honest and faithful expositor will find or make his work any easier than by textual or topical preaching, for it requires thorough and honest effort. But, it can be done, and when done well, an intelligent and devout hearer will be apt to feel that he has been addressed by the Lord more directly than in many other sermons equally true and effective." Our goal surely is to make the hearer feel that he has been addressed by the Lord.

The textual preacher counters that he is preaching the Word. This does not necessarily follow. Textual preaching may or may not be an exposition of the Will of God as expressed in the Word of God. We shall later take time to illustrate the means by which it may be exposition; but more often it is not. The text is far more often used as a springboard, which, having served as a pretext for beginning, is no longer used or needed. We would offer the advice given by the character, "Claude," a Protestant minister, in *The Preacher and the King*, wherein he says, "To be then a minister of the Word, take largely. It is a treasure open to all. It is the only book of which no one runs the risk of being accused of plagiarizing. Take! These ideas which have already belonged to so many millions of intelligences are as fully yours as if you had been the first to see them." As Fenelon says, on page 130, "The primitive bishop stood up and read the Gospel or some other portion of Scripture, and pressed on his hearers . . . a few plain and forcible truths from that portion of the Divine Word. We take a text and make an oration."

We assert confidently in concluding this portion of our preliminary thinking on this theme, and on the basis of these preceding assertions, each given weight by forceful quotation, that expository preaching, well done and fearlessly applied, delivered after the most careful preparation and complete study, will give the preacher that which he needs to make him a success in his calling. It will make him a prophet, for to speak the meaning of the Word, as inspired and explained by the Spirit of God, is to speak forth the message of God. It will properly arouse and use his emotional powers, for by having set his heart afire with the very Word of God he will properly communicate this emotion to the people to whom he ministers. It will guarantee to the preacher the needed note of authority, for that preacher who can preface and punctuate and conclude his sermon with "Thus saith the Lord" needs no other "props." It will enable the preacher to win his congregation to God, for the Word is the Word of God; and to be won to it is to love it and its Author, and to honor the expounder thereof for what he is, a mere tool and not an originator. It will guarantee success. Naturally we must properly evaluate the elements of success. By this we cannot mean the "biggest" (numerically) churches or the largest salaries or the greatest crowds. These may be valid as testimonials to the preacher's real power and success, or they may have little relation to it. (The greatest salaries, crowds and acclaim go to those in this world who amuse the populace, and not to those who instruct it.) We remind ourselves that we are sent to teach, to preach, and to make disciples, teaching them "all things." As we teach and preach the Word, the whole Word, impartially and fearlessly, we shall be teaching "all things," and we shall further find that souls will turn to this manna and be filled with the fulness of God.

In concluding this chapter we offer two more quotations. The first is from Dr. G. Campbell Morgan, taken from a personal letter in reference to this course and the general trend of its material: "I am quite convinced that (expository preaching) is exactly what the church and the world need, and that there is no substitute for it." The second quotation is from Dr. James Black, in *The Mystery of Preaching.* After careful investigation among lay men and women he reports,

> "I was astonished and pleased to find an almost unanimous preference for what we call expository preaching, where a text, passage, incident, chapter or book is chosen and its central truths expounded and applied. Even in America, where purely topical preaching has largely captured the market, I find this preference exists strongly among the most thoughtful people."

CHAPTER II

Basic Considerations

Someone has said that the pulpit has become so enamored of the analysis of our economic and ecclesiastical situation, to say nothing of personal needs and problems, that the preacher is in danger of becoming an amateur analyst of social phenomena rather than a man who brings a curative for these social ills. When a patient is ill he needs not only the diagnosis but the medicine. The Word of God has already correctly diagnosed the condition of man. In expository preaching we present the medicine that serves as panacea for all ills, personal, national, international, social, economic or moral.

He who is to become an expository preacher must discover and master a method. That prince of expository preachers, Dr. G. Campbell Morgan, says in a personal letter commenting on the material then in process of preparation for inclusion in this book, "In the discovery of method there is more value than in the gaining of information." The difficulty lies in the fact that expository preaching is not so much a science, but rather more an art. And yet, it is both at once! Strict rules and modes of procedure cannot be laid down. We can at best suggest and illustrate and leave it to each to discover his own best use of that which is suggested and illustrated as to methods. This is not to say that there are no fundamental and basic principles, for there are such. But, the application of these principles in the production of the completed sermon is a thing each must grasp for himself and use according to his own technique. It is as Dr. Knott (*Expository Preaching*, pp. 42-43) says (though he writes it concerning the "appeal" of a given passage),

> "The appeal . . . is determined by one of several factors. It may be the temperament of the preacher, the needs of the congregation as he understands them, his experience, or his understanding of the Scriptures. It is perfectly obvious that, since no two men are alike and the circumstances of no two congregations are just the same, no two men reviewing a portion of Scripture would use the same theme. . . . Furthermore . . . the development of each would be different. While all this could be true, THE PROCESS COULD BE THE SAME (caps ours)."

It is the process or method which we must master, and then apply, each in his own way. Methodology is necessary in every science and art. Preaching is a living thing, and the methods for the art of preaching may vary as need for varying applications of the art is seen. Preaching must be vibrant with life and reflect the age in which the preacher lives and to which he speaks; yet it must be scientifically prosecuted and withal in tune with the timeless message which has been given. And so we must master the various methods in order to do the best work in this "scientific art," if we may so designate this work.

This treatise is designed not only to say as so many have already so well said, "It ought to be done," but to declare the methods by which one may do it. Advice on two points must be considered by the tyro. First, let not the novice announce a long series. One ought not even announce that he is to preach expository sermons. Surely the announcement will bear no weight unless one has earned a reputation for good use of this method; and, unless the sermons reveal themselves to be truly expository, naming them so neither will make them so nor arouse interest. The second word of advice is that one ought to begin with the shorter books and simpler methods. This advice is given mainly for the reason that absolute familiarity is essential. The background, content and exegesis of the passage or book must be grasped clearly and known well before any preaching is done, and naturally the shorter books are better until one develops proficiency in this type of approach.

With all that has been said and yet will be said about method, either of approach or of final outlining, we still must say that we must never sacrifice the effectiveness of the sermon for the sake of conformity to rule or correctness of form. If there is spiritual power, the carefully and skilfully modeled sermon will be far more effective than the slipshod, clumsily fashioned one. We must further bear in mind that some passages of sustained beauty may be more effective when used as illustration and quotation than when dissected by exegesis before the people. A consecrated and alert imagination will discover means by which one can lead his people into a deeper study of these passages without destroying the continuity and beauty of the whole.

One must avoid seeking to sound clever in his sermonic formation or exegetical presentations. He must rather seek for simplicity and progress in unity. However, one must never be ashamed of actual ability. He must develop and use his powers to the limit, remembering all the while that prayer is the real secret of power. While immersed in prayer one discovers the very facts and factors that are most needed by the hungry and thirsty souls before him. The expositor, in common with the preacher of other types of sermons, will find that the hardest labor and the most sustained effort and deepest thought and most intense searching will all be well repaid.

The expositor will love the Word. He must make methods his servants and be slave to none. He must have (or gain) a "sense of the literature." He must have a lively and well attuned and completely consecrated imagination. He will have a theology, but it will be simple and broad as well as deep and sure. "The whole of the Word for the whole of man" will be his goal. There will be no "danger spots" in his theology, whether of outbreaking unbalanced fanaticism or of weakness caused by incomplete thinking.

The question may well be raised as to the need for a carefully wrought outline. We shall stress this need constantly, and it seems well here to declare the reasons. Methods of constructing outlines assuring variety and unity and arousing interest thereby, and other kindred subjects, may be found in any standard work on homiletics. It is assumed that those who press on to this type of work have already had the basic courses in homiletics which cover this ground so thoroughly. Someone has put it this way, "We must assure ourselves of real listeners — hence the value of subject and introduction. We must hold the attention — hence the value of outline." We discover that the outline keeps one from the danger of rambling, which is a particularly attractive, though a forbidden field in expository preaching. The outline is the track to a predetermined goal, truth or station. The freedom of the Spirit is usually more effective if it is kept within certain predetermined bounds. The outline makes a tempered wedge out of the raw ore. A sermon must have unity and progression to be effective, and it cannot have these essential characteristics unless they are carefully built into the outline.

And so we shall proceed to the discovery of scientific methods of producing artistic outlines for the preaching of expository sermons. We love the Word, and those to whom we shall preach it. We use the expository method to bring the one to the other, seeking only the glory of God thereby. It is not our task to read into these pages any of our own interpretations, or to make its stories and teachings come to the aid of our own preconceived notions. Our task is to bring our own thinking and all of life to its illumination. Thus and then we shall discover truth and be enabled to obey the command, "Preach the Word."

The expository preacher might well heed "The Preacher's Beatitudes." The original author is unknown. They have appeared under many guises, yet with but slight variation. They do not, of course, solely apply to expository preaching, but they are nonetheless valuable to us for that.

1. Blessed is the preacher who knows how to preach.
2. Blessed is the preacher who shortens his introductions.
3. Blessed is the preacher who modulates his voice and never shouts.
4. Blessed is the preacher who knows how and when to stop.
5. Blessed is the preacher who preaches at himself.
6. Blessed is the preacher who preaches on great themes.

Basic Considerations

7. Blessed is the preacher whose sermons are articulated and progressive.
8. Blessed is the preacher whose sermons are a unity, with a definite aim, and every superfluous word cut out.
9. Blessed is the preacher who sometimes allows the congregation to sing an entire hymn unexpurgated. (Why not get the time by expurgating part of the sermon?)
10. Blessed is the preacher who rarely uses the pronoun "I." ("I shall read OUR lesson.")
11. Blessed is the preacher who knows that the object is the end and the subject only the means to the end of the sermon.
12. Blessed is the preacher who knows how much of the sermon he is responsible for, and how much he may and must leave to the Holy Spirit.
13. Blessed is the preacher who is called of God, and called TO PREACH.
14. Blessed is the preacher who, having fully surrendered his life to God, is inspired of the Holy Spirit and anointed with power to reach souls for God and to educate them once they are saved.

To these we would like to add another. This may be implied under No. 6, but we would like to state it. "Blessed is the preacher who preaches positive sermons." We are not here to expose or tear down or deny. We have a positive message, and the sooner we prosecute our primary task the sooner Satan's power will be broken and these things against which we often joust like Don Quixote will be revealed as but "windmills," and lacking enduring substance and being unworthy of the effort we would expend to oust them.

In concluding this chapter and as a final word, we reaffirm our assertion that no one without a deep and abiding love for the Bible as the Word of God should, or indeed ever can, preach expository sermons. We must love it as the saints and martyrs did, and embrace it in its entirety rather than life itself. It is not only our textbook, it is our very life, our power house, our universe. Upon this we insist, not because of Bibliolatry but because we have no other material to which to turn, and this has proved itself dynamic in every fair trial.

THE BIBLE

(Three short stanzas out of a longer poem)

"O Book! Infinite sweetness! Let my heart
Suck every letter, and a honey gain.
Precious for any grief in any part;
To clear the breast, to mollify all pain.

"O that I knew how all thy lights combine
And the configurations of their glory!
Seeing not only how each verse doth shine,
But all the constellations of the story.

"Stars are poor books, and oftentimes do miss.
This Book of Stars lights to Eternal Bliss."

— GEORGE HERBERT[*]

---

[*] George Herbert was not only one of the metaphysical poets of the seventeenth century; he was also one of the great English preachers of that century.

CHAPTER III

What Is Expository Preaching?

or

Discovering a Definition

Having approached our study with the consideration of the important foundation facts and factors, we press on to the direct investigation of the subject of expository preaching. Again we lead up to the substance of the matter by several considerations. We must remind ourselves at the outset that to call our preaching expository and to have it really that are often two very different things. We must first discover how to do that which we desire to do before we can claim to be doing the desired thing. But before we turn to positive definitions there are some valuable facets of our theme to be considered.

Expository Preaching Characterized

Expository preaching is the door to much hard work. Of all expositors whose writings we have read, not one but has expressed his positive conviction that more work and harder work is necessary to the accomplishment of this type of preaching than in topical or textual preaching. Therefore we must emphasize that no man who is afraid of earnest mental and spiritual application should even attempt this kind of work. At the first, four or five times as much time will be required for the preparation of an expository sermon than for other kinds. True, this will not forever be the case. Practice makes for ease and proficiency, but never will this be a "short-cut" way, nor can it ever be for the lazy man a successful way.

Expository preaching is the door to a deep and abiding satisfaction. Isaiah records the promise, "My Word will not return unto me void." This promise is especially precious to the expositor. Even apart from this promise we have testimonies in a veritably continuous stream, testifying to the value and helpfulness of this kind of preaching. Our Lord never promised that OUR words would accomplish fruit-bearing, but assured fruit when HIS Word is sent out. This is literally fulfilled, thus heightening the satisfaction of which we have been speaking.

Expository preaching is the door to an educated constituency. I well remember once calling upon an elderly lady who was ill in the hospital. She was not a member of the church of which I was pastor. She had moved to the community a few months before and had been attending this church quite regularly. She said, "I have been a member of three churches, covering a period of thirty-eight years. These have always been Baptist Churches. I always have attended quite regularly, but I have never really known what I believed or why until I have sat at your feet and listened to your sermons on 'John.' " (And this was in the earlier years of my attempts at expository preaching!) We are told to "be ready to give to any that ask thee a reason for the hope that is in thee," and it is readily provable that expository preaching will prepare our people (and ourselves as well!) far better than any other kind or type.

Expository preaching is the door to a consistent freshness and variety in preaching. This is not so in any other kind. If this were not a necessary condition it would not be so consistent. Neither would expository sermons be so constantly pertinent as testimony affirms that they are. The best part of this pertinency, freshness and variety, is that the preacher need not be particularly conscious of it, especially the pertinence. Once I was preaching as a guest preacher on a summer Sunday. In the Word was recorded an ascending scale of godliness. The word "patience" came in turn. Almost in passing I touched on this word urging patience with youth by age and with age by youth. After the service a lady came to me and reminded me of this part of the sermon. It seemed that her little son had been determined to brace his feet against the back of the pew before them. His grandfather had been annoyed by this and kept forcing the little feet down. Both were about to forget where they were when that point in the sermon concerning patience came in. The grandfather listened, looked sideways at the grandson, and allowed the little feet to stay braced. The little fellow cocked his head, listened, gave his grandfather a sly look, and allowed his feet to hang down nicely for the rest of the service. This is a very homely illustration of how in greater and sometimes in more ticklish ways the Word is constantly pertinent, though the preacher is not at all conscious of it. The Word simply yet powerfully presents its many-sided message.

Expository preaching is a door to a unique type of preaching for America. So many express a liking for it, comparing it to a cool breeze on a hot day or some other similar comparison expressive of pleasing uniqueness in the sermon. The almost fruitless attempt to find literature giving instruction in the construction of expository sermons is another proof of its unfamiliarity in this country. And so almost without the authority of research, we approach this unique but most desirable and valuable method, which is fundamental to all worthy preaching.

We have said that expository preaching is the door to hard work, and that it takes longer to prepare an expository sermon than any other ordinary kind. Now we present another truth which is not as contradictory as it may sound. That is that *expository preaching will save time for the preacher.* This is of course not in reference to the individual sermon, but in other ways. There will be no scurrying for texts or topics, and hence precious hours will never be wasted in the attempt to settle the then vexing question, "What shall I preach about?" Spurgeon, who is regarded by some as a foe to expository preaching, makes a sad confession to his students. In Vol. I, page 136, writing concerning the choice of a text, he says, "I frequently sit hour after hour praying and waiting for a subject and this is the main part of my study." (For that individual sermon, we understand.) We dare submit that such sitting and waiting, even with prayer, is both a waste of time and of nervous strength. However, Spurgeon was more of an expository preacher than he realized and much more so than his critics credit him with being. We quote from *Life and Letters of C. H. Spurgeon* by Needham, page 43, wherein Needham quotes a correspondent from a Baptist newspaper: "A gentleman informed me that he had heard Mr. Spurgeon preach his first sermon here about sixteen years of age: he then read, prayed and expounded the Word." Then, see Mr. Spurgeon's sermon, "On the Cross after Death," page 98 in Vol. XVIII of his sermons, and find a pure diverted-expository type. He tells the story, presents the exegesis, and then proceeds to build his sermon on the prophecies thus fulfilled. Also see page 235 in the same volume, "A Bit of History for Old and Young." Then see in the volume containing the sermons of 1885, sermon No. 2, on page 29, "The Rocky Fortress and its Inhabitant," a good sample of the microscopic expository approach. Also, read his lectures to his students, volume on "Commenting and Commentaries," the opening paragraph beginning, "In order to be able to expound the Scriptures . . ." and then on page 34 favorably quoting Bengel, "Put nothing into the Scriptures, but draw everything from them and suffer nothing to remain hidden that is really in them." We have no space to go deeper into this argument, but mention these facts just to show that Spurgeon was much more favorably inclined to what we call "expository preaching" than some are willing to admit.

Expository preaching will even save time for textual or topical sermon preparation, for texts and topics will crowd themselves in upon our minds clamoring for treatment. And, as we progress in this kind of work we shall discover that each sermon of this type, well prepared, helps us in the preparation of other sermons of this type, though on a passage or truth. The Word grows on one and becomes a well of springing water, bubbling up and running over, perennially fresh, thirst-quenching, and satisfying to preacher and to people alike.

As Dr. William Stidger says, in an article entitled "The Bible as a Basis of Great Preaching," posthumously published in *Church*

Management (Dec. 1949, page 9): "The Bible has never failed me. I have never opened its pages since I have been in the ministry that I have not turned to a text that has gripped my soul. One need never go outside of the Bible for preaching unless he desires. In its single text, in its poetry and parable, in its drama and fiction, in its human interest story and its historical pageantry, in its prophecy and its preaching, it is inexhaustible."

Expository Preaching Defined

But, if expository preaching is all this and does all this, just what is expository preaching? Exposition means to set forth the meaning of ... or the purpose of ... this time "Scripture." It is a setting forth of the subject matter without immediate reference to the critical arguments about that matter. Note the word, "exposit." "Posit" means to "place." "De"posit means to place safely away. "Ex" posit means to take out of place and reveal to view ... to take out of obscurity and place in light.

John Hall, in the Yale Lectures of 1875, says,

> "Expository preaching does not mean a rambling paraphrase, so as to hit current events ... nor a devout meditation ... nor a subtle ingenuous twisting so as to disclose vital truth ... nor extensive spiritualizing of the text so that every part means something else ... nor a godly talk concerning a certain chapter which begins nowhere and ends at the same place. By expository preaching we mean that in which the minister ... has learned what meaning the Holy Spirit intended to convey in a passage ... and then what uses he ought, in harmony with the rest of Divine teaching, to make of it. And having filled his own understanding and warmed his own heart with the truth, tells it to his people with clearness, force, and fervor."

Somewhat to the same end is a quotation from Henry Ward Beecher, in the Yale Lectures of 1872. He says, "The Word of God in the Book is a dead letter. In the preacher the Word becomes again as it was when first spoken by prophet, priest, or apostle. It springs up in him as if it were just kindled in his heart, and he were moved by the Holy Ghost to give it forth."

Expository preaching is designed to deliver to the hearts of saints and sinners of today the entire message of God as He gave it to men of old. Therefore, the whole Bible is regarded not only as our legitimate field but our necessary field, which we must at some time preach in its entirety. We may not slight any part of it. We must bring men the whole counsel of God. It is not enough to bring a phrase from that counsel and in its light attempt to interpret the mind of God toward men and their affairs. This may be a valuable message, but it is not the exposition of the will of God. On the other extreme there is the prevailing idea that expository preaching means a discourse on a chapter, from verse to verse, *ad sereatam et infinitam,* thus making the sermon similar to a commentary treatment of that passage. Both views — the purely partial and the extreme-minute — are false, yet both contain some truth. The expositor may present a minute study of one verse, or a bird's-eye view of the whole Bible, and he is still the expositor provided that in his presentation he presents not his own or others' conclusions, but the Will of God as revealed in the portion under scrutiny.

Exegesis, while a necessary and inevitable background to every expository sermon, is nevertheless only that background. We might say that the exegetical study is the finding of the brick, and the expository sermon is the completed building. Exposition does not include the process of the discovery of the details of the matter to be expounded, but only the helpful setting forth of that matter to the hearer.

The ways of expository approach to the Bible are possibly as many and as varied as the men doing the work and their combined minds. But whatever the specific method insofar as the completed sermon is concerned, let us re-emphasize that exegesis and exposition are inextricably related, and always in one way, i. e., that EXEGESIS IS ALWAYS, WITHOUT VARIATION, THE PARENT OF EXPOSITION. An expository sermon is far more than an exegesis. Exegesis, as we have said, is the brick. It may even be also the mortar. But the expositor in preparing his sermon has taken the brick and mortar and given

What Is Expository Preaching?

to them line and color and temporal meaning and relationship and design and purpose and perspective. We use the brick and mortar before us; but in the pulpit we present not a hodge-podge, but a completed sermon. An exegesis begins at the first verse of the passage under consideration and ends at the last, considering of course sources and purposes. An expository sermon begins where the hearers are and ends, after going through the ascending truths, illustrations, arguments, and passion, to a place predetermined in the mind of the preacher by the message of the passage under consideration. To acquire the facts is exegesis. To set them forth in a form both intelligible and interesting and profitable to the listener is exposition. What we are trying to say is that we must always have a "sermon." We obey the rules of homiletics and utilize all the principles we have learned. Our product must be of such nature that as a general rule the man who is not interested in Bible study and does not know an expository sermon from a Moa bird will nevertheless feel that he is being given a sermon, complete in and of itself. But at the same time the Bible student will revel in its disclosures and implications and follow avidly the various portions of the passage as they are touched upon. He recognizes the "brick" for what they are. The former man only admires the completed building, not caring about the architect's specifications and minute details.

CHAPTER IV

The Exegetical-Expository Sermon

This study of the exegetical-expository method is included in Part One because it is *the* fundamental approach. No one will ever become an expository preacher who does not master this chapter, or at least the method it sets forth. A firm grounding in the disciplines of this basic approach will serve as a guard against some of the dangers which will be noted in the applications of this method as those applications are presented in Parts Two and Three.

Three Dangers

In some of the studies which we shall later present there will be evident a great similarity to other of those studies and in some instances the differences will be rather striking. Each application will however be presented as though it were a separate "method" and so supported. We assume the right so to present and defend each application as a method; for while the exegetical expository method is the foundation of all, there are varied ways of progressing beyond that foundation. Let nothing we shall later say lessen our emphasis on this one basic approach and the details presented hereunder, but on the other hand let us not be satisfied with the monotony that will result if we do not progress to the various possible applications of this method.

It is due to the fact that would-be expositors have been circumscribed by the false idea that this approach is the only one, and furthermore, because this work has not been done well, that expository preaching has fallen into disrepute in many quarters. We must overcome this negative attitude; and our emphasis that this is the basic type of expository sermon, and that yet there are many

The Exegetical — Expository Sermon

possible approaches of this method, is calculated to overcome this attitude. Experience has proven that our contention is defensible.

Each type of sermon we shall consider is as much a type of Expository Sermon as is each other type. Many factors both within the Scripture and within the mind of the preacher will demand the differing approaches. Of these we shall later speak.

If we were to be asked how we shall determine the type of approach to be used with different kinds of passages we should not be able to answer directly and positively. The choice of type is decided by a "sense of the literature" which will come only with study and practice. There can be no specific rule in this matter. Some passages lend themselves to several types of approach, the choice depending entirely upon the mind of the expositor at the moment. Some naturally unfold themselves in one method or another. The student who is constant in his efforts and search will soon be able readily to discover, without rule or direction, which type to use in a given case. If we were merely to present the exegesis of various passages, of course there would be no problem, for the treatment of each would be the same as all others. But, though exegesis is the foundation, the parent, the necessary precedent to every expository sermon (as we have already said in preceding pages) exegesis may be a dry and detailed delineation of things or ideas. This may be of value, but it may be and probably will be dry and of little general interest. We desire therefore not an exegesis, nor yet merely a sermon, but an exegetical-expository sermon. It must be truly and fully exegetical, yet truly homiletical in its final form and presentation. It must truly teach, but teach by indirection and suggestion more than by direction and information, though in this type of preaching the latter is often utilized.

Apart from the danger of considering this the only type of expository sermon, there are two other very real dangers. These warnings could be repeated under every type, and we shall doubtless refer to them again, but surely they must be called to mind at this point. The first of these dangers is that we shall serve our guests a plate of hash instead of a full dinner of a predetermined number of courses. We must guard against producing a commentary in the pulpit. We must be sure that each presentation is really a sermon, with properly balanced structure, a definite and challenging start, a progressive development, and a valid conclusion.

The second danger is in reference to a dangerously easy carelessness. One is apt to get careless in any mode of sermon preparation or in any other phase of ministerial work if he is not constantly on the watch over himself; but the danger here is particularly acute and the results of falling prey to it are devastating. It is easy to arise on comparatively short notice and say some very nice and indisputably true things in reference to words or phrases in a chapter or passage. There are always the dear old "aunties" (male or female, it matters not) who are so ready to praise every effort (however abortive) of their dear pastor, doing it with more charity than discernment. Woe be unto the would-be expositor who breathes this monoxide gas! No preacher may slight any detail of conscientious preparation without being guilty of venial sin, and repetition soon makes this verily into mortal sin. Beware, then, the dangers, but welcome the opportunities of this type of expository preaching.

The Exegetical-Expository Method Illustrated

For our example of this method we take a portion that readily lends itself to this kind of approach, the twenty-fourth chapter of Matthew, verses 1-14. The eschatological implications of the passage and of our outline of it may be entirely disregarded and the illustration will stand, nevertheless. We know this chapter quite well. We have read it, studied it, defended or doubted or criticized it, but now we want to preach a sermon on it.

Our first task is a deep and broad familiarity with the Gospel. This task may for the present stand as an ideal rather than an immediate requirement. By this we mean that if we were to defend our exegesis of the passage this total familiarity would be an essential. For the present purpose, the study of method, we need not go into the full background, but turn immediately to the study of method.

Assuming this then as an ideal, yet disregarding it for our practical purposes, we press to *a second step which is to become thor-*

oughly acquainted with the passage. We should approach the passage afresh, as though we had never seen it. This may be hard to do, especially with familiar passages like this. This can and it must be done. The reason is that "A little learning is a dangerous thing." It is so easy to read over words or ideas upon which our minds have never lighted, and thus we easily miss some point that will be of real value to us. A good way to do this is to read the passage aloud, as though to a child or a person who knew nothing about the Gospel story.

Correct Scripture reading is exceedingly difficult. At this point we practice carefully correct reading, for we must read the passage with such clear thought and such proper emphasis that the tones and inflections of the voice convey the full meaning, without any interpolation whatever. This type of almost "children's story" reading will be found to be most helpful.

Naturally we assume that we have approached the Book in a spirit of prayer, not only general prayer, but specific prayer for this very need. We shall read the passage not once or twice, but several times ... it may be a dozen, twenty-five, or if necessary fifty times. We shall not memorize it, yet we shall become so thoroughly familiar with it that when we see the first verse we see also the middle and last, and when we come to the middle we see the first and last. That is, not a general familiarity, but absolutely a mind-picture of the whole. Whatever the cost we must attain this familiarity.

Now then, being in general quite familiar with the Gospel, and being specifically and in great detail familiar with this passage, we are ready to begin our written work. We read again, verse by verse. At the end of each verse we pause, and then write down on paper opposite the number of that verse a word or two that will express what to us is the leading thought of that verse. Sometimes one word will suffice. Sometimes several will be needed, but as a general rule the fewer words we use the better off we shall be. Naturally, this will mean a careful re-thinking of every verse.

Now we move to *the next step, the vital exegetical step.* We read the passage in the Hebrew or the Greek, or at least trace it carefully through a good commentary or two or three. As Dr. Stidger says, in his article already quoted, under division VI of his article, headed "How to Use the Bible in Preaching."

"Know it in the original if possible. Know the Hebrew and the Greek. There is no perfect substitute for this knowledge. However, if one has not had the privilege of knowing the Bible in the original languages there are innumerable commentaries and dictionaries for his use, from which he may approximate a knowledge of what certain texts and passages mean through second hand knowledge of specialists."

"Each word, intonation, tense connective, preposition, adjective, verb — every single iota of each verse must be mastered. Dr. Jeff D. Ray, *Expository Preaching*, P. 28 bases his work *almost* entirely on the English Bible, and emphasizes for us at this point the need of and value of grammatical study in exegetical work. He says that a rather random effort by even the tyro will disclose this. He says, 'The Bible abounds in passages where the meaning hinges on grammatical construction.' "

We shall of course take notes during our study and investigation. These notes will be on a sheet of paper or several sheets, not using the sheet on which step one is recorded. Thus we go through the passage, having at the conclusion of our study one piece of paper on which is a list of the verse numbers we are studying, and also a column of words or phrases expressing in as brief form as possible the thought of the whole passage. We shall have on other paper a whole mine of facts and ideas and suggestions, many of which we will probably have to discard insofar as this particular sermon is concerned, but the gathering of which has by no means been a waste of time. We shall have not a record of preconceived notions, but a genuine first-hand exegetical study. Our paper on which we have the column of words is our basic homiletic workshop, while the other material is our brick, wood, steel, etc. The first list will show the development of the chapter. Our past and consistent general, though minute, familiarity with the chapter will immediately group certain verses together if they do not come together in order. We shall have discovered a topic or theme. (In this we see a great difference between the spirit of the expository preacher and the textual or topical. The expository preacher discovers what the Scripture talks about, and preaches about that. Most others choose their theme and enforce that from such portions of Scripture as support it, or they get support elsewhere.)

Now we are ready to work on another piece of paper to *draw our rough outline.* Here we place the topic that has been revealed to us. Under it we put the groups of verses that we now see belong together, in the order of main divisions . . . giving these groups a topic of their own, though recognizing that this topic may, of course, be but temporary. Now we insert under these main divisions the necessary sub-topics, not as we develop the theme in our minds, but as our exegetical study and word listing have revealed sub-topics to us. Each main heading must have reference to a group of verses, and each sub-topic should have reference to a verse, in part or whole, or perhaps more than one verse. Not one leading thought may come from other than the actual teaching of the passage.

Next we proceed in accord with good homiletical rules for any sort of sermon. Having thus prepared our materials and having arranged them in such order that a purpose and a developing relationship are seen, we decide upon the goal and write the conclusion. Having thus established and having phrased the goal, we can return to the materials to discover which of them is the nearest to where our people probably will be at the time of the delivery of our sermon. This decision will determine our introduction, so we now phrase that. Knowing now for surety the goal and the starting point, we can readily arrange the divisions of the material in an orderly and progressive manner.

Now we are ready to "polish" our outline. We should rewrite and rephrase our topic if necessary . . . our main headings if necessary, and also restudy our subheads. They should finally be in such form that the main heads could almost be written after ditto marks under the topic. The sub-headings ought to be quite easily handled, in the same manner as the main headings. Here we are homiletes, producing out of our exegetical "brick" the completed building, balanced and framed and beautiful both to look upon and listen to, if we may so mix our metaphors.

The result will be a truly homiletical outline, with Topic I, II, III, and more if necessary, with 1, 2, 3 (and again, more if necessary), and even under the 1, 2, 3, sub-subheads of a, b, c, if needed. Our most important steps in the development of our theme are the Roman numerals. Next in order of importance come the Arabic numerals. Next in order come the letters, and some go so far as to have still further designation of sub-sub-subheads. Now, due to some unforeseen arrangement of the service, is there twice as much time as you planned to have? Then develop fully the sub-subheads. Or, is there half as much time? Just leave out the subheads! Nothing important to the main thought will be left out. There is still unity and progression, and we still have a real sermon.

But, we have said little about all the work that was done in exegesis! This will be used to a very large degree. First, it will help us with our subheads, and then with our sub-subheads. It will at times furnish most interesting illustrative material, new, up-to-date, fresh and instructive. Here is nothing "cut and dried." Here is no danger of any charge of "plagiarism." Here is a note of originality in our sermon, so much to be desired as a goal!

Finally, we have our complete and fairly full outline. From this point in we leave our work to the usages of the individual preacher. Some wisely write all their sermons in full. Some brood over them and practically "mind-write" them. Some just fill mind and heart with the general theme and specific material and then preach what is called "extemporaneously" from the notes. *Let each do with this outline what his own experience and training has taught him is best for him.* Our opinion is that surely a preacher ought at least frequently to write his sermons. Surely he ought to brood over them, and "preach out of the overflow." And just as surely he ought to be able to preach extemporaneously and yet follow his outline as he has predetermined, in order to reach the desired goal.

An Outline Illustrating the Exegetical-Expository Method

We present an outline based on Matt. 24:1-14 for illustration of what can be done with this method.

The Exegetical — Expository Sermon

It will be noted that we deal with only the first fourteen verses of the chapter. This is done for two reasons. First, the use of this part the better illustrates the method. Second, this illustrates how careful preparation for expository preaching will save time. We have from verse 15 through verse 51 to preach upon later, and there is much ground in which those who read their Bibles will be interested as they note that which will come later! We could cover the whole chapter, but this would be very difficult to do in an exegetical-expository manner, in a sermon of ordinary length. Therefore, instead of preaching on "His Coming," and considering in one sermon the entire chapter, we use the title, "Before His Coming," and use that portion of the chapter that applies to that title; namely, the first fourteen verses.

For introduction we picture the scene of verses one to three, and connect that with the natural query of the Christian mind of today (and even of the non-Christian mind, also). Connect with 23: in thought: the human Jesus never entered the temple again! (Vs. 2, maybe, "do you not yet see all these things, i.e., cf. 23:36-39.)

I. CHRISTIANS MUST NOT PERMIT THEMSELVES TO BE LED ASTRAY AS TO THE FACT OF HIS COMING. The Parousia assured — (ref. Acts 1:11, 3:20.) Vss. 4-8.

1. We are warned of false Christs. Vs. 5
   Not necessarily using name, Messiah, but usurping His position and authority — "in my name," better *on*, i. e., on the strength of.
2. We are warned of tribulation. Vss. 6-7.
   Wars and political confusions and conflicts.
3. This is only a beginning. Vs. 8.
   Odinon — rather "birth-pangs" than mere "sorrows"

II. CHRISTIANS WILL SUFFER WITH AND FOR CHRIST BEFORE HIS COMING. Vs. 9.

1. "Deliver you" . . . falsely accuse . . . betray.
   Then — not a specific time, but a development of sorrow unto sorrow, a step, a degree.

2. "Kill you" . . . physically, spiritually, socially.
   Deliver — afflict — kill.
3. "Hated of all nations." (Sounds like attitudes today in many nations.)
   N. B. — "For my name's sake." (Not mere refusal of our interpretation of Him, but hatred of His very Name.)

III. CHRISTIANS WILL LIVE AMONG MANY MISUNDERSTANDINGS BEFORE HIS COMING.
   (Then — another step or degree. Not a special time.)
   1. Each thinks he is right.
      "Christians" deliver "Christians" to the tribunals.
   2. This makes for confusion, worse confounded.
   3. No egotism like the religious.
      "Hate one another" — opposite to "Love one another."

IV. CHRISTIANS WILL BE TORMENTED BY FALSE PROPHETS BEFORE HIS COMING. Vs. 11.
   1. This will mislead many.
   2. True Christians will not follow them. (Some folks follow every new cult.)

V. CHRISTIANS WILL SEE CLEAR LAODICEANISM BEFORE HIS COMING. Vs. 12.
   (Because of apostasy.)
   1. This is suggestive of our own day.
   2. Iniquity abounds, and men say, "Where is the power of this Gospel?"
      Not only sin but *anouia* — apostasy.
   3. The love of many therefore waxes cold. (True Christians are not mislead)

VI. CHRISTIANS WHO ENDURE WILL REJOICE AT HIS COMING. Vss. 13, 14.
   1. Endurance itself brings a reward.
      Endurance — antithesis to apostasy.

2. Full salvation guarantees endurance, and vice versa.
Sothesetai — "shall be saved."

Conclusion: Missionary activity, in person or with group, guarantees against failure and dry-rot. "Witness!"

Appeal: We are still in the time "Before His Coming." Are we "enduring" and waiting and watching? Keep busy for Him, and there is nothing to worry about. And then shall the end come, *telos* (consummation of purpose?).

It may be desired to bring in vs. 15 in the introduction, and use the rest of the chapter as filling and illustration, thus bringing the message of the whole chapter. There is danger here of making the sermon too long on the one hand, or of making it too much like a Bible study period on the other. The decision to use this material at this time would depend on the temper of the people to whom the sermon was to be preached, and of course each pastor knows his own people best. For the beginner we would advise the approach illustrated here.

In order that the student may practice the method here described we suggest (or assign) another passage for similar treatment, Mark 2:13-3:6. In order that we shall not deny him the privilege of untrammeled original work, we place our suggestion of one way of outlining this passage in the appendix. See Appendix Number 1, page 127.

Part II

APPLYING THE EXPOSITORY METHOD TO SELECTED COMPACT PORTIONS OF THE WORD

Introduction to Part II

In many ways some of the several methods presented in Part II are not of themselves distinct methods, but only variations of the one basic method, as varying kinds of Scripture demand such variatin. And yet, they are real methods, in spite of that fact. The outlines illustrating the various methods do not always reveal in themselves the differences between the various methods. The description of the method, presented in the explanatory part of each chapter, will reveal the differences as well as some likenesses. This explanatory part presents ways in which certain passages may be handled, explaining thereby also how other passages of similar spirit may be used for sermon bases.

The progression from the "microscopic" (dealing minutely, as under a microscope, with one verse or two) to the "telescopic" (dealing broadly and inclusively with an entire book of the Bible) may at times seem to be by minute steps. This seeming is factual. The gradations are frequently not broad. Careful study and several years of experimentation and of teaching have revealed them to be real gradations with each method truly helpful to that person who would obey the apostolic injunction and "preach the Word."

CHAPTER I

The Microscopic Method

An expository sermon and a true textual sermon are basically the same, save that the former usually deals with a longer passage of Scripture. Having said this in no wise assures that the sermon based on the shorter passage of Scripture will truly be textual. The true textual sermon is one in which the text is dealt with expositorially, or "microscopically." A sermon which merely "has a text" does not classify as a true textual sermon.

The true textual method is a part of any good system of homiletics. Probably more sermons have been prepared with the textual method in mind than any other method. We include this method in a book on expository preaching, because, as we have affirmed, the true textual method is truly expository — the preacher using a microscope, as it were, because the portion he studies is comparatively minute.

This kind of sermon can never be mistaken for a topical sermon. This kind of sermon is always rich because true texts are rich, and the text very naturally furnishes the structure and design as well as the theme and topic. The text even furnishes the best of illustrations and appeals! This kind of sermon seems, as one views merely the outline, to be very simple and easy. It is neither simple nor easy. Careful study is demanded at every point if we are to be true to the text exegetically and also true to the sermon homiletically.

Not every verse of the Bible is a true "text." Not every verse can even serve as a textual basis for a topical sermon! But a true text for a true textual sermon must be one of such content and structure as to allow for this kind of treatment. For, of course, every branch or brace or support or suggestion will come directly from the text. This will mean that no other text will do for this sermon, and no other sermon will do for this text.

The context must be studied and weighed. No text may be taken out of its context, ever, for any pretext. In the full light of its setting the text must be studied so one may discover its true import. In the light of the truth, the text must now be placed under the exegetical microscope. The good student will use the text in the Hebrew or Greek at this point for translators translate words but the preacher must assuredly translate ideas and interpret all implications. All English versions are good at certain points; all fail at some points. The expositor may not fail. He must as carefully dissect and analyze this verse as a research chemist would dissect and analyze live tissue. Nothing may be "read in"; no content may be left out. Every shade of meaning must be grasped and interpreted and related to the whole verse.

In the process of this dissection the three general vital portions of the true text will be discovered. The main thoughts will be seen, the supporting factors or arguments will be related to the main thoughts, and all items of value as illustration will be understood. The preacher will work with extra note paper at hand. Here he will jot down all ideas as they are discovered. From this "pile" of material he will now proceed to form his sermon, using the best techniques of homiletics to get unity, clarity and progression.

The resultant outline frequently looks like something which has been simply arrived at. The labor of the exegete may not show, but by the correctness of all implications the preacher will be protected from all errors, and in the touches of new information the value of the research will be seen.

For our illustration of this method we use John 3:3. We find in this short text a great wealth of material. Every word is important and must be studied carefully. Finally, after having done the required work we gather from our note sheets the following outline:

Topic: "The Inescapable Imperative"

Introduction: We do not like imperatives, yet life is full of them; we may disobey, but a true imperative inexorably exacts its price

The Microscopic Method

for such act. A term more technical and more correct than "inescapable" would be "categorical." "Inescapable" shows the correct idea — it is unconditional. There is no "if," no "perhaps," no loophole to this imperative.

I. The speaker, having unconditional authority, undergirds an unconditional imperative. (ref. Matt. 28:18. "All authority has been given unto me.")
   1. The positive affirmation of the speaker. *"Amen"*—repeated, firm.
   2. The speaker, "I." The root, the center, the reality of Christianity.
   3. The very word with which He prefaced His imperative is strong — "Say."

   Not *eipon*, mere "words," but the strong *lego*, "Verily, Verily I say."

II. The imperative rests with equal burden upon all who would qualify for the predicate.
   1. The predicate refers to the unspoken yearning of Nicodemus. He was not concerned with "teacher." He wanted eternal significance.
   2. All normal hearts have this same goal.
   3. To *all*, then, — "Unto you" — and not only to Nicodemus, the imperative rests. Ye must be born again, else — be denied the predicate.

   Ou dunetai idein — is not ever able to cast a glance upon. *idein* — "glance," not the strong *horao* — "To study and search out."

III. The demands of this imperative.
   1. "Born again," anew — true. *Gennethe anothen.* "From above" signifies the source of and given power to "again" or "anew."

2. Upon us therefore rests this imperative, unconditional — "be born from above" if we would in the slightest degree enjoy the predicate — "see the Kingdom of God."

Conclusion: Inescapably reminded of Paul in I Cor. 15:50 — "Flesh and blood cannot inherit the Kingdom of God." Ye must be born again.

For a second study of this method we assign a text which is so big as to be too big — and yet with this approach this truly great text can be put into normal sermonic length, to the great blessing of preacher and hearer. We therefore assign John 3:16. For the illustration of how this text may be handled, see Appendix II, page 129.

CHAPTER II

The Paragraphing Method

The method of expository sermon preparation to which we next turn our attention we call "paragraphing," a title which comes from the method of handling the passage in the early stages of the development of the sermon outline.

To illustrate the method we have in mind we turn to Matthew 8:18-34. First we read the passage, trying as in the exegetical expository method, to read it as though we had never seen it before. We continue this reading, trying not to memorize the chapter but to gain a complete mind-picture of the whole. We must be sure to get so complete and detailed a picture that as we read one verse we discern the interrelationship between that verse and all related verses in the chapter or portion. We want to see it as a mental picture, and note all of the interaction of the various parts. This may seem very easy, but we are so used to seeing certain relationships that we shall find that unless we are very careful we shall pass over others that are quite important.

Thus far we have proceeded as for exegetical-expository preaching. We shall later investigate into the minutiae of the passage, but at this point we change our method. Instead of putting down on paper every verse, phrase, word, inflection, for careful study and exegesis, we strive to state under one general heading as many verses as possible. We jot down, therefore, not a long list of words, but in just about the minimum of words by this "paragraphing" process, we discover the main development of the passage. Done superficially this becomes so easy to one who gains a sense of the literature that unless he is careful he will be sorely tempted to stop here, make a sermon outline immediately, and do no further exegetical study. Against this failure the preacher must be on guard. There is needed here just as careful exegetical study as under the exegetical-expository method. Every word and phrase and inflection must be understood to the best of our ability. All available avenues of investigation into meanings and interpretations will be followed assiduously, and all possible new ideas discovered. However, before we go to this careful exegetical study, we do here, in this method of approach, draft our first rough outline, making it of course on the basis of the "paragraphing" already done with such care. After this comes the exegetical study. We must be careful lest we make the finished product too exegetical, which of course this type of sermon does not permit. This outline will be smoother, more flowing than the exegetical-expository. It is calculated to capture the interest of the person not normally interested in Bible study, as well as to hold the attention and interest of the Bible student. Passages of less detailed content and more of inspirational worth will usually suggest this method of treatment.

It is difficult to illustrate on paper just what we mean by the "paragraphing" and the relation of the rough outline to the completed outline with the exegetical work as intermediary, and still to keep to the fore the difference between this and the exegetical-expository sermon. The preached sermon will show the difference immediately in that the illustrative material and "filler" is not so directly an outgrowth of the exegetical study. Careful procedure in preparation will reveal it to the students. The mechanics of the "paragraphing" must be within the genius of the individual preacher, for no rule can be laid down for our guidance. We shall of course bear in mind that the expositor is the teacher-preacher. He will therefore watch for opportunities to teach, not in the exegetical-expository way, but by illustration and indirection. He must give not "lessons," but tasty "tid-bits," attractively handed out in passing and as illustrative material. This is, in fact, a most effective kind of teaching.

Before coming to the place where one is ready to mold his final outline after this method, the preacher will have before him three sheets of paper. First will come the rough "paragraphing." Then will come the rough outline, at the head of which in all probability he will insert the theme which the passage has by now revealed to him, although if this wait until later no harm is done. The third sheet will be his real "pile of bricks," for out of that carefully selected exegetical material he will ultimately build his sermon after the pattern revealed in the paragraphing — using the brick not for its own sake but to beautify and portray more vividly the details of the paragraph-headings.

Now then, we are ready to present our outline. We select as our topic, "Following Jesus." For our introduction we "set" the passage. Luke records vss. 18-22 as taking place later, in the Perean ministry . . . the rejection by the Samaritans "because His face was as though He would go to Jerusalem." Then, James and John want to call down fire on the village, but Jesus rebukes them and goes on to another village. Then comes a man, who says, "I will follow thee, Lord, but first suffer me to go and bid farewell to them that are at my house." But Jesus says, "No man, having put his hand to the plow and looking back is fit for the Kingdom of God." The rest of this story Mark and Luke also record as taking place at this time.

In this story, then, there are revealed facts and implications concerning "Following Jesus," as revealed by Jesus Himself.

I. THE FOLLOWER OF JESUS CAN HAVE NO OTHER PRIMARY TIE. Vss. 18-22.
   1. "Jesus," the God-man, Messiah, makes the conditions clear. ("Son of Man" here equals "Son of God.")
   2. "My Kingdom . . . not of this world" . . . is the reason.
   3. "Hath not where to lay His head."
      Not a matter of extreme poverty and privation, for "the laborer is worthy of his hire." Rather, here it is self-forgetful service that is required. (It is not easy to follow Jesus. Must break all other ties.)

II. THE FOLLOWER OF JESUS IS THE FOLLOWER OF A MIGHTY CHRIST. Vss. 23-27.
   1. The fierceness of the storm is well attested. These were fishermen.
   2. The sleeping Jesus gives force and occasion to the timidity of the disciples. Had he not been sleeping, perhaps they had not been afraid!
   3. Note: "Great storm" . . . "Great calm."
   "Oh ye of little faith." (Should they have let Him sleep, and felt assured just because He was THERE? Do not storms often make us the better because we have silently endured? Hard to tell how far to carry this idea.)

III. THE FOLLOWER OF JESUS IS THE FOLLOWER OF AN UNWELCOME CHRIST. Vss. 28-34.
   1. Power over evil . . . to cast it out . . . not really desired.
   2. Material profits are the only canon in this world.
   3. As men have treated the master of the house, so they will treat the servants. (Usually they make it a bit worse!)
   4. Luke reports that this man wanted to follow, and Jesus sent him back home to be a missionary.

Conclusion: Are we ready to follow? To break all other ties? To wait patiently for Him to use His power, and trust in any case? To follow an unwelcome Christ? Then, if the challenge is great enough, accept it and find the life that ensues full of challenge and deep satisfaction.

For a second study of this method we assign Matthew 21:1-11. Our suggested outline on this second portion will be found in Appendix III, page 131.

CHAPTER III

Spiritualizing

This chapter, which presents what we must call "spiritualizing," is a chapter of three basic divisions. Originally we avoided the use of the word "spiritualizing," because it has been abused. We had three separate methods presented in three separate chapters. However, as we continued to study and then explain and also discuss in classes these which at the first seemed to be three distinct methods, we came to a conviction that they are three possible ways of applying one basic manner of Bible teaching, "spiritualizing."

As we have said, our word is in poor repute. It is a good word, but it has been wrongly applied. Too often in spiritualizing a text the real content is effaced and only a "spiritual lesson" is left. Surely it is proper to draw spiritual lessons from the Bible. Some passages have the greatest practical value to us when studied with this purpose in view. On the other hand, it is as surely not proper to deny, or imply the denial, of history or prophecy. There is real danger in uncontrolled spiritualizing. Every good thing is subject to abuse, but wise men do not abandon a good thing because fools abuse it.

We present three ways of spiritualizing, or, of drawing out a spiritual message. Each has a particular and peculiar value. Each is somewhat similar to the others and yet has its distinctions. As can be said concerning most other methods, the type of Scripture passage selected will probably determine the manner of treatment.

A. Diverting a Text to a Worthy Purpose

This which we call the "diverted" method, is a method whereby one takes a clear presentation of Scripture truth and "diverts" this into channels of spiritual or practical application. There will be little if any exegesis in the sermon, although we shall of course use what we desire for illustrative purposes. The procedure for this method is not so much mechanical as spiritual and "pastoral." One reads and thoroughly digests the passage, seeing "all the configurations of the story." The lenses and prisms will adjust his spiritual eyes to lights and colors — that is, the passage, having been fully and intimately grasped, becomes a telescope through which the preacher looks at life. Then he talks, not about the telescope, but about that which is revealed to him. Or, we might say that one stands on the heights presented by the Scripture story, and looks off to its general or specific spiritual implication or moral application. In the use of this method we do not deny the plain meaning of Scripture, whether history or prophecy. We admit and enforce by defending and applying therefrom a message for our own day. We make a direct practical application. We divert, legitimately and deliberately, the primary historical or prophetical purpose of the Scripture passage to our own temporary needs, meeting the needs of our congregation thereby.

This method can only be used with full effectiveness in relation to familiar stories, or such stories as can be related quickly and quite readily carried in mind throughout the sermon. ✦ Usually the Scripture lesson embodies the story. That is not necessary, though strongly advisable. Our purpose here is less the didactic, as far as the Bible record is concerned, and more the hortatory. As usual in expository work teaching will be included, in passing and by indirection.

In order to illustrate this method we study and prepare an outline from Matthew 20:1-16, a very familiar parable. It may seem that we are suggesting a way to deal with parables. This is true, to a certain extent, but not fully so. We have deliberately chosen a parable for the illustration of this method, so that in presenting the method of dealing with parables in a later chapter the student can readily see the difference. Also, this is a good opportunity to illustrate the overlapping of methods, and to reaffirm our assertion that very frequently the same passage will lend itself to several modes of treatment. However, we proceed with our outline, first having fully familiarized ourselves with the passage in the whole and in all of its parts. This will mean that we shall have to do some commentary-reading, and possibly discover other sermons preached on this portion so as to get all of the "slants" that it is possible to get. Here surface familiarity is not enough, although our exegetical study may not relate itself directly to our theme or our outline.

Our introduction will relate this familiar parable as briefly as possible to cover the important points of the story. We note that it was occasioned by Peter's question, Matt. 19:27, which had to do with rewards, and that Jesus proceeds to speak, not so much of the rewards as the basis for granting of them. It is easily seen that this is a question easily roused in the minds of Christians, indeed usually there already, and attention is gained at the outset.

I. GOD ALWAYS FINDS WORK FOR WILLING HANDS. ("Why stand ye here idle?")
  1. "Give new members a job." . . . (Are they willing?)
  2. Some people get busy about something . . . others have to be asked and teased.
  3. At least, be willing, and do not haggle over the wages.

II. GOD PAYS ALL HIS LABORERS. ("I will give what is just.")
  1. Salvation is not the reward for good works, but the result of faith.
  2. There is more than MERE SALVATION offered to the Christian.
  3. "It hath not yet been revealed what we shall be." In other words, reward is coming, surely, to all who work.

III. GOD PAYS, BUT NOT ON THE BASIS OF LABOR ACCOMPLISHED. HE PAYS ON THE BASIS OF FIDELITY TO OPPORTUNITY.
  1. We compare disciples of first century, Paul, Peter, John, and ourselves.

2. We compare preacher and teacher and leader with ourselves.
3. Neither precedence nor amount of work accomplished will be the deciding factor. Some have greater opportunities and abilities. We must be faithful to grasp each opportunity as it presents itself.

Conclusion: No value in railing at God's grace. Cannot have any pride in position. The lowliest saint, if faithful, is as obedient as the more prominent one. (Maybe more so.)

(This is not an excuse for slothfulness and indolence, in pulpit or pew.)

A passage for the student to use in further exercise on this method is assigned, Matthew 15:1-20. Our work on this passage is recorded for study and comparison in Appendix IV, page 132.

B. Illustrating Life by an Apt Text

This method illustrates rather obscure Bible truth by holding up against it well known principles as revealed in the life of our day — or it illustrates rather obscure present world conditions by holding up against them some well known or readily explained Bible passage. We use the entire passage and the entire sermon to do what is done in every other sermon, i.e., we "illustrate."

In sheer mechanics this method is at the first almost exactly like the "paragraphing." It differs from the paragraphing in that its aim is not to dwell on the sections of the passage but rather to use those sections as illustrative of life or reveal them as illustrated by life.

Our background of preparation is the same as for other methods — namely, (1) full acquaintance, (2) careful exegesis, and (3) a full understanding of the surrounding of the passage. Then we prepare as for a "paragraphing" outline. We place alongside the sections of the passage the conditions of our day which demand attention, conditions on which these sections will throw light. It is this step which makes all of the difference as between these two methods.

Spiritualizing

In a very real sense we are spiritualizing. We are drawing forth from the passage a spiritual lesson for our day. Our exegetical work will be of great value, for we shall soon discover if we do not already know, that the very words of Holy Writ are up to date and alive with meaning for our own day.

Usually in the sermon we shall spend half of our time in presenting the passage, and then the other half in presenting that which it illustrates. (Or, half of the time in presenting a problem of life, and then spending the other half showing how this passage throws light on that problem.)

For illustration we turn to the first chapter of the Lamentations. Most of the prophetic writings lend themselves to this treatment. Their messages were given to their day, and had to do with their actions and especially their relation to their God. It is easy to see that these messages, simply interpreted for THAT day, are not sufficiently challenging, but if we can interpret them to our day or interpret our day in their light, then they may well be invaluable.

It might be well in this instance to present the introduction before we read the Scripture lesson. In this introduction we could "place the book," describe the tenor of it, and the spirit of its author. If then we read it with deep feeling and strong oratorical power, the very reading of it would have great meaning to our people. Else, in fact, they might well wonder why we read such a passage, and why we are so wrought up over it!

The topic which we choose for our message is "The Bleeding Heart."

Introduction: We have read the DIRGE of Jeremiah. What does this reveal to us?

I. IN THIS CHAPTER WE SEE THE BLEEDING HEART OF THE PROPHET.
   1. The desolate condition of Jerusalem. Vss. 1-6.
      a. Solitary and alone. Vss. 1, 2, 6.
      b. Gone into captivity. Vs. 3.
      c. Not even anyone in the temple. Vs. 4.
      d. Her enemies supreme. Vs. 5.

2. The cause of this desolation. Vss. 7-11.
   a. "Jerusalem hath grievously sinned." (Worship of Astarte, etc.) Vs. 8.
3. Useless to appeal to the world for aid. Vss. 12-17.
   a. "Is it nothing to you, all ye that pass by?" Vs. 12.
   b. "Zion spreadeth forth her hands and there is none to comfort her." Vs. 17.
4. The justice of this judgment. Vss. 18-20.
   a. "The Lord is righteous, for I have rebelled against His commandment." Vs. 18.
5. The only comfort Jeremiah can find is vss. 21-22, the enemy is likewise to suffer!

II. HEARTS HAVE CAUSE TO BLEED IN OUR DAY!
   1. The world is desolate. (Spiritually, economically, socially, racially, etc. etc.)
   2. This condition is caused by SIN.
   3. Appeal to world force is useless. (League of Nations, U. N., agreements, etc.)

Conclusion: What is our outlook? The prophet saw no hope, save comfort that the enemy would likewise suffer. Jesus once wept over Jerusalem, but that moment he offered no hope. However, because Jesus WEPT, and DID SOMETHING ABOUT THE CONDITION, we today may have HOPE . . . HIS BLOOD. And, as our hearts bleed for the world around us, we can and will offer to them this hope — namely, THE BLEEDING HEART OF THE CHRIST.

In order that the student may study to apply this method we assign for his consideration the second chapter of this same book, Lamentations. An example of dealing with this passage will be found in Appendix V, page 134.

C. Portraiture as a Backdrop for Exposition

Much of the Scripture is in picture language, and many of its chapters present a picture the homiletic value of which is greater if regarded as an object of admiration and adoration than if treated as a subject for dissection in the sermonic laboratory. In this method we take a passage that patently presents a picture. We approach it not for its details but for its whole impression. Here a study of art or of art appreciation is most valuable, and the phrases of the art-student can well be utilized in our study; lines and solids, lights and shadows, contrasts, entrances and exits, perspective — for here the preacher is more the artist than the scientist. To illustrate as we describe the method, we turn to the Revelation 1:9-20. We study the passage as usual. It might, of course, be treated in other ways, exegetical or selective for example. But the passage presents to us a glorious picture, and we desire to make our congregation see the same picture. This is a most difficult thing to do. One can describe some things rather easily, but to so describe a picture, which is as yet in words, so others can see the same picture, is quite difficult. We have suggested that a study of art-appreciation is valuable in the use of this method, but a lively and consecrated imagination will solve the problem. This imagination will first enable us to see the picture as a picture and not as a story, and then it will enable us to transmit that picture and its message to others through the ear and heart gates; for we must not only enable them to see it, but also to grasp its great message. It is not as we merely hold our congregations that we can be said to succeed, but as we place their feet on higher and firmer ground. And so, our word-painting must be a sermon, and this method guides us to success in this matter.

Only so much exegetical background as is essential will show in our finished work, for our purpose is description and impression rather than teaching. However, details of exegesis are extremely valuable, for our picture must be clear-cut and not hazy in any of its details. One must so carefully study the passage that he can close his eyes and see the picture. The size of the frame, the objects and their sizes, where each person or object would be on the canvas: almost a rough crayon outline of the basic content of the picture.

The title of our picture is "Christ in the Midst." For emotional introductory material this writer told the story of an unlettered peasant standing enraptured before a painting (at a "Station of the Cross") in a French Catholic Church (in France during the first World War). We recalled his tears and the deep emotional bearing evidenced as he left the little church. The value of a picture lies not in its cost, but in its emotional content.

I. THE DETAILS OF THE PICTURE BEFORE US.
   1. The seven-fold Candlestick (One stand, seven candle holders).
   2. The Son of Man!
      Flowing robe . . . golden girdle . . . white hair . . . fiery eyes . . . feet, burnished brass . . . voice as many deep-flowing waters . . . countenance like the sun.
   3. The seven stars in his right hand.
   4. The two-edged sword — out of his mouth. (Thy Word is sharper than a two-edged sword.)
   5. The Word, I am the last, etc . . . . (One with God, who is Alpha and Omega.) "I have the keys." (Who said Peter?) The mystery explained.

II. THE MESSAGE OF THE PICTURE.

Dazzling picture. Finally see Christ in the midst of His church, which is One though seemingly divided.

The purpose of the church . . . not to display inherent unity nor to call attention to herself, but to provide a stand or station where the Light of the indwelling Church may freely shine forth.

The light which the Church sheds . . . reflected. As church is composed of members, so she will shed that light only as the members do.

The place of the church in the program of God . . . Central. Cannot neglect without peril.

Notice the sword . . . the Word . . .

Conclusion: Gain the blessedness of this message, and avoid the warning. Come into the church.

Spiritualizing

The student will readily observe a great similarity to both the "illustrative" and the "diverted" methods. These are all "spiritualizing" as we have asserted. Yet there is a basic difference (especially as comparison, this method will be "illustrative") and that is in the spirit in which the passage is handled. Perhaps the word "impressionistic" would apply here, but certainly it would not apply in the "illustrating" method. This method is perhaps in many ways more truly "spiritualizing" than either of the other two methods presented in this chapter. One must be very careful lest he destroy the historic or prophetic values in the passage thus treated.

For assignment for further study we suggest Revelation 4:1-11. Our work on this passage is recorded in Appendix VI, page 135.

CHAPTER IV

Selecting the Desired Ideas Out of a Passage

Again we come to a method which is one of the "easy" ways of preaching an expository sermon. We call this method the "selective," taking the name from the mechanical forming of the outline. The fact that we do thus "select," insofar as our final outline is concerned, and the fact that a ready and glib talker can often make a show of more full preparation (though not constantly to the same congregation), makes this a method one that must be used only with care. Yet, there are times when one will deliberately desire to use this method, not from laziness but from purposeful choice. The true expositor will prepare as carefully as though he were planning to preach an exegetical-expository sermon. Looseness in preparation, here or elsewhere, easily degrades an expository sermon into a series of pious platitudes — using a passage for a pretext, instead of a text for the same disgraceful purpose. Sometimes a passage will demand this kind of treatment, but more often the method will be chosen because of certain "high spots" which the preacher will feel led to present.

In a way we may say that the selection is purely arbitrary. By this we mean that we have no special rule to offer that will serve as a guide in selecting. It may well be that no two would select the same items out of a chapter, or even that the same man will wonder, a while later, why he ever made the selections he did instead of the ones that now challenge his attention. But on the other hand, there are some helpful ideas that one may utilize in the decision as to what he will select. Perhaps certain nouns, or verbs, or prepositions or conjunctions or names or adverbs or what-not will stand out. In this case the selection may not be so purely arbitrary, in a way; and yet, of course, the fact that one chooses the verbs, for example, instead of the adjectives in a given passage, is based on pure arbitrariness and on no particular rule either of homiletics or demand of the passage itself.

When the selection finally is made, the ideas may be presented either in chronological or numerical or logical order, or sequence, just as the preacher may determine. He will use the entire passage only insofar as the headings or subheads determine, being careful not to use much that may seem to be very good material, but for the time being is outside the scope of the preacher's theme. The preacher will quite surely avoid leaving out anything in the passage that is truly pertinent to the general theme of that passage, or on the other hand of going in the slightest contrary to the whole message of the Gospel. We may select portions, but the way of treating the portions must invariably be in tune with the whole. We have no more right to wrest the meaning of Scripture here than has anyone else anywhere else. We must preach the whole of the Word to the whole of man, and it is not a question of whether we like a certain slant which the Scripture reveals or whether we do not like it. We are to preach truth, and that truth as revealed in the Word. Naturally we cannot in every sermon, nor in many years of preaching, present the whole of truth. Therefore, selection is permissible in a sermon even as one sermon is a selection out of the whole body of truth. But, we must never run counter to the implications or demands of the whole.

Familiarity with Hebrew or Greek or both will here show its great value. Of course one will scarcely ever be a worthy expositor without these two languages. But in this method the preacher will be enabled to bring out shades of meaning and emphasis where mere translation will not so do. Of course, we shall not parade our knowledge or make pretense of possessing that which we do not possess. But, possessing it, surely we ought, with due deference to the demands of the occasion, make use of our valuable tools.

But now as to the details of the procedure. First comes the usual "first-reading," and then the re-reading for general and complete familiarity. Now we decide what ideas we desire to select out of the passage. We jot these down on paper. Now we study the passage, both to enlarge upon these ideas and also to check carefully, asking, "Am I using all that really belongs to these ideas, all that is needed to bring out the complete thought of them?" And, "Am I in any sense or place wrongly interpreting the whole?" When this study is completed, we will dismiss that which is not pertinent and proceed to place the material set aside into such order as we desire. Now we will select . . . or rephrase if we have already visualized . . . our topic. Under that we will inscribe the outline . . . and use for subheads or illustrative material only such of our selected material as is needed. Many interesting items will be passed over at times, perhaps, but there is always plenty left, and there are many times when these minor items will be quite usable, for illustration in other sermons, or for textual sermons.

To illustrate the sermon outline resulting from this approach, we turn to II Timothy, the second chapter. Our theme, "Vessels to Honor."

Introduction: Discuss "of" and "to" honor. World desires to be "of," and the Christian "to" honor. The question often is, "How?"

I. BE CLEAN. Vs. 22.
Negatively . . . "Flee"
Affirmatively . . . "Follow"

II. BE HARD. Vs. 3.
Christian life is a warfare.
Hard training "toughens" one.
Singleness of purpose gives grace to "stand the gaff."

III. BE COMELY. Vs. 15. Unashamed
Approval must be to God.
True comeliness is of soul and not face. ("The eyes have it" . . . and "The eyes are the windows of the soul.")

IV. BE TEMPERED. Vs. 1.
Strengthening is a growing and progressing process.
The stress required in tempering but strengthens the metal.
The source of the grace that provides both means and patience in this process.

Conclusion: Vs. 11. "Faithful is this saying . . . for if we be dead with Him . . . we shall also LIVE with Him."

For a further study of this method we assign a consideration of Acts XVI, which allows for this kind of treatment. For our second illustration of this method, turn to Appendix VII, page 137.

CHAPTER V

The Devotional Method

The devotional method is one which seems to be very easy, but this is only a seeming. If it is easily done, it is most likely because it has not been well done. In general this method is more like the exegetical than any other, yet it is also very similar to the "grouping." It differs from the exegetical in two very important items. For one thing, we have no real outline. And here lies a seeming simplicity which is at once also the greatest danger-point. Having no outline, we may be like birds on the wing . . . but with nowhere to go especially. We may rove all over the meadow and get to no place and accomplish nothing. But, there are times when we do not, as in the ordinary sermon, desire to get anywhere. We want only to make people meditate along certain lines. Our problem is to have no specific outline or generally discoverable "progression" in our sermon, yet get people to meditate along the certain lines we have in mind.

This type of message is especially valuable at mid-week meetings, or, at special occasions such as Easter sunrise, or Passion week, or Christmas. This is also a fine way for us to bring to the people indirect preachments. A chapter may contain many elements our people need to consider, yet be difficult to organize. We do not desire to preach a "selective" sermon. What shall we do? We present a "Meditation" on the passage. We may not desire to say very much about those certain things we have in mind, yet some reference to them is desired. So then we plan a short series of "Meditations," or seek a special occasion when this chapter can be used to advantage, and in a kind and quiet and effective way present those matters that are upon our minds. We shall find that for producing a desired result at certain seasons, or for presenting "sore" matters, few methods equal this one. Surely no offense can be charged when the Word is allowed to suggest ideas! Preaching might give the preacher wider scope, and he might step too hard on the sore corns, but a meditative outline and spirit enables us the better to keep control over every phrase and thought and still allows a direct leading by the Holy Spirit.

But, we go on to discover the other difference from the exegetical sermon. The first was its lack of what is ordinarily considered an outline. The second is that there is very little if any exegesis in the sermon, and here lies another genuine danger-point. For, while there is no exegesis in the sermon itself, there must be the same exegetical preparation behind the sermon. It is advisable, however, to prepare the general flow of thought in the chapter ... call it an outline or whatever you choose, *before* the exegetical work is done. This will aid in keeping a devotional atmosphere, where otherwise it might develop into an exegetical sermon or some other kind. We shall frequently find that our outline, or "running comments" based on more than one verse, yet not broad as the "grouping" process, will frequently lead us to a climax. Surely some kind of climax is essential, but just how it is to be reached and handled each must decide for himself.

We have said that there will be very little if any exegesis in the sermon, but this must be modified somewhat. There will be exegesis, yet it will not clearly be seen as such. All interpretation and explanation is exegesis, but the exegetical research will not be evident. The similarity to the grouping method will readily be seen, but the difference lies in that under this method we take smaller portions, and do not try in any sense to express as many verses as possible under one group heading. For an example of this method we present an outline based on Matthew 23.

Topic: "Are We Pharisees?"

Introduction: Vss. 1-2, Jesus tells who the Pharisees are, and where they place themselves. "In Moses' seat." Cf. Nh. 8:4a and 8b, "Ezra the Scribe ... read in the book of the Law of God distinctly, and gave the sense, and caused them to understand the reading." The scribes were then "givers of the sense of the Law." But, though they taught well, they did not live what they taught, (Vs. 3) and, they bound on heavy burdens, but gave no help, (vs. 4).

- Vss. 5-12. Inordinate pride . . .
    - vs. 9 . . . R. C. Church!
    - vs. 10 . . . Masons! "Worshipful Master."
- Vs. 13. Dogs in the manger.
- Vs. 14. Pretense of religion to cover irreligion.
- Vs. 15. Even lead converts astray.
- Vss. 16-22. Wrong judgments of right and wrong, permissible and nonpermissible.
- Vss. 23-24. Part-way godliness.
- Vss. 25-28. Putrid within in spite of fine exterior.
- Vss. 29-31. Religious show is not religion.
- Vss. 32-33. Children must suffer, too, unless converted.
- Vss. 34-36. Carries out vss. 32-33.
- Vss. 37-39. The Passionate Jesus! God angry at sin . . . but never vindictive. Are we Pharisees? Yes! Are we sure that we are white within, and that we live what we preach? The letter killeth . . . the spirit giveth life . . . be sure to judge rightly as to what is right and wrong, etc. Be sure our religion is no mere show!

We are "Pharisees" (Religionists of our day), but LET US NOT BE "PHARISAICAL."

For a second study of this method we assign Matthew 27:24-66 as a passage to bring to our sermonic laboratory. For our second illustration of this method, using this Scripture portion, turn to Appendix VIII, page 138.

CHAPTER VI

The Telescopic Approach to a Given Book

This method stands between two approaches. That is, we may approach the whole Bible, and determine to preach a telescopic sermon on its natural parts or divisions, the book, each as a unit in itself; or, we may approach any separate book, and determine to preach one telescopic sermon in this whole unit. For these reasons this chapter stands at the end of Part II, and immediately before Part III. It should be obvious that while Bible-book sermons are very satisfactory, in spite of the evident and very real difficulties, no study of any part is well done without a complete background of the whole of which it is a part. We separate the individual book from the whole for a purpose, but we must see and bear in mind that whole.

This approach is most difficult to illustrate. In fact this may be said of every method proposed! And this difficulty arises in every case from the same cause — namely, because that which one sees through his "telescope" demands far more on the mind behind that telescope than that toward which that telescope is directed. That is, different persons may study a given book, and decide upon different key-verses, leading verses, climaxes, etc., and each may reach a perfectly defensible conclusion. We must begin with the conception that every book in the Divine Library has a purpose. This purpose may be hidden or implied in presentation, and difficult to state definitely and finally. But purpose there is nevertheless. The discovery of this purpose will lead to a sense of the whole, and this, as we have said, is necessary to an understanding of the parts of that whole. In every book, whether story, argument, song or prediction, there is ethical appeal. Information is given for inspiration, discussion to aid in choosing direction, and vision to the end that virtue might accrue. Ethics is the science of ideal humanity, and ethical intention is revealed all through the Bible. History was not given for the sake of giving information concerning yesterday, but to give us a clearer understanding of God and at the same time inspiration concerning how to live today. Prediction is not given to satisfy our curiosity about tomorrow, but to enable us to live virtuously today in view of that tomorrow.

Our first task is to master the content and structure of the book and grasp its purpose. Some books lend themselves easily to structural study, and some are more difficult. We must master the book no matter what expenditure of time and mental and spiritual energy is necessary, for we are the only ones who will bring the message of God to His people.

We shall take for our first illustration of the telescopic approach a book in which the purpose is very evidently declared, the Gospel according to John. After we have read and re-read the book, so that we see it in our mind's eye almost as clearly as John himself saw it, we proceed to dissect the book. We discover its mechanism, its main teachings, its varied lines of thought, its arguments to support its main contention or contentions, until the center or "key" is made clear to us. In this case the discovery of purpose is not difficult, for it is clearly stated "These are written that ye might believe . . . and believing . . . have life in His Name." John then has set about declaring and proving something about Jesus, something which, if accepted, will lead to life. This something can only be one thing — namely, the deity of Jesus of Nazareth. And so we study the book, to find out how John goes about proving his declaration. We find that John refers to "signs" in such a way that we cannot escape the significance of the word. So we mark down references to all "signs." We grasp their purpose as well as content, and their relation to the whole purpose of the book. We put down also references not directly concerned with signs, and try to discover their relation to the plan of the whole. Ultimately a marvellously well-balanced outline is revealed to us. We discover that all signs are grouped under three heads: Words,

Works and the Fulfillment of Prophecy. We discover that there are eight under each heading, and that the material or stories not connected with "signs" are also in eight portions. This matter is preceded by a prologue and followed by an epilogue, each of which is closely related to a brief historical reference, one referring to the opening of Christ's earthly ministry, and the other to the closing of it. Finally, we have the book reduced to framework, and in this framework we discern the design.

We see immediately that though our preparation for this sermon has been tremendously involved, there has been a great gain in it all, for each portion of the book before us cries out for exegetical treatment. We have thirty-seven sermon portions all ready for treatment! In this as in the preceding methods we shall discover, if we have not already, that the expository preacher not only preaches but he also teaches. His teaching is made to seem incidental and is therefore all the more acceptable to a congregation. Any congregation loves to discover facts not before seen, but they do not like school-room methods of presenting these facts. If the facts are "sugar-coated" by being buried in a lively and moving sermon, they will be very happily received. So then we decide to include these very interesting facts in our sermon, not as mechanical outline, but as sermon portions or divisions. We shall not directly call attention to the mechanics of the book, but let the mechanics show just enough to be of interest to those who are definitely interested in Bible study. Our sermon, then:

Topic: "The Declaration of a Dynamic Deity"

Introduction: The prologue . . . in brief. But, today men question the full Deity of Christ, and also belittle His avowed purpose! (As revealed in 3:16.) The purpose which John declares, "That, believing, ye might have life through His name," declares a dynamic Deity . . . Deity with a purpose and power to accomplish that purpose. And so, we say to John . . . "Very well, prove your contention." So John answers . . . Listen!

I. THE WORKS THAT JESUS DID DECLARE THAT GOD WAS WITH HIM, FOR "NO MAN DOTH THESE WORKS SAVE GOD BE WITH HIM." What works?
   1. Turning water into wine. 2:1-11.
   2. Cleansing the temple. 2:13-22.
   3. Healing the nobleman's son. 4:43-54.
   4. The man at Bethesda. 5:1-47.
   5. Feeding the 5000. 6:1-15.
   6. Stilling the storm. 6:16-21.
   7. Healing the man born blind. 9:6-11.
   8. Raising Lazarus. 11:1-16 and 33-46.
   (Growingly more suggestive of Deity. Note that seven of the eight are in the first half of the book.)

II. THE PERSONAL AFFIRMATIONS OF JESUS DECLARE THAT EITHER DEITY OR DEGRADATION MUST BE AFFIRMED.
   1. I am He. 4:1-42.
   2. I am the Bread of Life. 6:22-71.
   3. Before Abraham was, I am. 8:54-59.
   4. I am the Light of the world. 9:1-41 (except vss. 6-11, used in 7 above).
   5. I am the Door. 10:1-18 (Includes, "I am the Good Shepherd").
   6. I am the Resurrection and the Life. 11:17-32.
   7. I am the Way, etc. Chapter 14.
   8. I am the true Vine. 15:1-16, 23.
   (Growingly more deep and intense. Almost entirely in the center portion of the book. Dividing the book into groups of 5 chapters. Surely these are affirmations of Deity on the part of Jesus.)

III. THE DELIBERATE ACTS OF JESUS IN REFERENCE TO THE FULFILLMENT OF PROPHECY DECLARE HIS DEITY.

The Telescopic Approach to a Given Book

1. These prophecies refer to the Messiah, where any reference is given.
2. Jesus deliberately claimed them as referring to him, and as proving his claim to his position.
3. These prophecies and their fulfillment quickly glanced at.
    a. "They hated me without a cause." (Ps. 35:19) 11:45-57. Cf. 15:25.
    b. "The King cometh unto thee . . . lowly and riding upon an ass." (Zech. 9:9) 12:12-19.
    c. "Unto Him shall the Gentiles seek." (Is. 11:10) 12:20-36 and 46-50.
    d. "Who hath believed our report?" (Is. 53:1) 12:38.
    e. "Yea . . . mine own . . . friend . . . hath lifted up his heel against me." (Ps. 41:9) 13:18-30
    f. "Numbered with the transgressors." (Is. 53:12) 19:18.
    g. "Cast lots upon my vesture." (Ps. 22:18) 19:23-24.
    h. "In my thirst they gave me vinegar." (Ps. 69:21) 19:25-30.

(Note: These are almost all in the latter portion of the book. Both by direct inference and claim they definitely proclaim Jesus of Nazareth as the Messiah, the Incarnate God.)

Conclusion: John records the last great sign . . . as if any more were needed! But he proves beyond a peradventure his claim that Jesus was God manifested in the flesh. The last sign? The resurrection.

Appeal: What of it if Jesus was God in the flesh? "That ye might have life in His name."

The objection has been raised by students that there is so much material that it is impossible to deal with this outline in any normal sermon time. To this we answer that we have presented this in one message of twenty minutes' duration, and we have also presented it at another time when forty-five minutes was available. One adjusts the amount of detail, study and reference to the time at his disposal.

A second study in this method, based on the book of Jonah, will be found in Appendix IX, page 139.

Part III

APPLYING THE EXPOSITORY METHOD TO THE ENTIRE BIBLE IRRESPECTIVE OF ITS NATURAL DIVISIONS

Introduction to Part III

In Part I we presented the basic considerations necessary to a correct vision of expository preaching, including therein that basic method, exegetical-expository, which is the heart and life of all expository preaching.

In Part II we applied this basic method in several ways, illustrative not only of technicalities in method, but inherently also illustrative of the way in which the preacher may with profit treat the passages which seem to demand or at least allow for such variety of method.

In Part III we shall apply the expository method to the entire Bible in the sense that we shall disregard the natural divisions of the book. In this portion of our study we are discovering methods which from the point of technique are no more difficult than those we have already mastered, but which are manifestly more difficult in that they require a broad acquaintance with the entire Bible. This acquaintance every preacher should have or delight to acquire, for he has the task of preaching the whole counsel of God to his people.

CHAPTER I

The Selective Method

In Part II Chapter IV, we considered a method which had this same title. We thought long over the use of the word again; we used other phraseology in class, in order to distinguish this from the former in the memory of the student. We have called it by various titles, all including some form of the word "concordance," for it is to the concordance one goes for help. But one does not exclusively use the concordance.

In the former chapter we were considering the expository method as applied to a rather short portion of Scripture, probably about a chapter. Within this limit the preacher selected such ideas as in his judgment set forth the teaching of the passage. He disregarded much of the passage insofar as inclusion in the sermon was concerned, although as a true expositor he would carefully exegete the entire portion.

In this present chapter we are presenting a way of preaching the Word based on several selected portions or verses or ideas from all parts of that Word. This might be called topical preaching. We include it under our general theme of expository preaching because if handled rightly it is the development of the topic in accord with the whole teaching of the Word and not in accord with only such light as the flickering candles of human wisdom can give. This is one good way of preaching doctrinal sermons, but whereas doctrine will be included in many other approaches and other than doctrinal sermons will be developed by this method, we cannot so label it.

Actually what happens is that the preacher determines his theme and then searches through the entire Divine Library for its teaching on that theme. The selection of the theme is arbitrary, but from this point on he is the expositor of God's truth on it rather than the teacher of his own vagaries or even "wisdom."

For our first illustration of this method we take the subject, "Prayer." We do this deliberately because the later chapter (Part IV, Chapter I) will deal with preaching based on those portions (brief, compact portions) which are actually prayers. Comparison between these two methods will help to clarify both to the student.

Probably the first step is to turn to the concordance (hence the possible title for this method, "Concordantial"). The preacher will put to valid and practical use the wealth of consecrated labor that has gone into the forming of these pages. The expositor cannot afford to be lazy in research, but neither can he afford to waste time and duplicate labor on mere gathering of factual material when others have done it for him. We should find a wealth of references to prayer, but of course the expositor is not limited to that which is noted in the concordance! In many of the passages he must include in his study, the word "prayer" is not used in any of its forms. (Hence we cannot rightly call this the "concordantial" method.) It is out of the expositor's broad knowledge of the Bible that many of his best references will come. As we have before affirmed in various ways, such knowledge is essential to the expositor.

A selective process is now essential, and here again a broad knowledge of the book is required. If one lack that knowledge he might be led astray. Surely he will not reach so great a height in expository preaching without it as with it. All of the references will be studied carefully so that all of the passages that illustrate factors in prayer or refer to the causes or processes or results of prayer will surely be included in those we select for basic treatment. Our selections are arbitrary, yet we may not so select as to produce a result which will even slightly swerve from the harmony of the true Biblical teaching.

Having selected our basic portions, we now review them so as to grasp from them an idea. In other words, a further selection is necessary. We still have too much material. If we had not gathered

The Selective Method

so much in the first place, we might have been biased. We have honestly tried to avoid all bias. We sincerely try to be true to what the Word says, in spite of all of the necessary arbitrariness.

Ultimately we select the following stories because from among all the passages studied these appeal to us as being true to the book when thus put together. They also make their own "appeal" to us in the usual homiletic sense. We select first the story in Genesis 18:23-33, wherein we are told of Abraham pleading with God for Sodom; but it is all to no avail, the city is to be destroyed. Then we turn to Deuteronomy 9:9-26. In this passage we see Moses on the Mount for forty days and nights, fasting in the presence of God. Then comes the sin of the people, followed by revelation of God's anger, and Moses' intervention. Again, forty days and nights of fasting and prayer before God gives in and agrees not to destroy the people for their sin, but to give them "another chance." Now we turn to Matthew 15:21-28, that story of most peculiar action and words from Jesus in His contact with the Canaanitish woman. What a problem this passage is! Our fourth selection is Mark 10:46-52, the story of blind Bartimaeus who is finally healed by Jesus. Then in close connection we come to Luke 11:1-13 and 18:1-8. In the one we are told by direct inference that no begging ought to be necessary when we are dealing with our Heavenly Father, and the other teaches that importunity in prayer is praiseworthy, for "Men ought always to pray, and not to faint."

Having chosen these portions, we place them before us. Six or eight Bibles open at once on the desk of the expositor ought not to be an unusual sight. We study these stories again, and read them over and over, until our minds and hearts are steeped in them. There are revealed to us here certain ideals and ideas which will finally form our sermon, though as yet we do not know which to choose. Our final goal is not exegesis of these passages; but we begin here, for we must have all the facts before us. Every sentence, every thought, every inference, must be clear in our minds, regardless of whether or not we intend to use them in our sermon. We see immediately that we shall again have far too much material to use, but we persevere just the same. Now, beside our conclusions as to exegesis, we set down our ideas as to the outstanding messages these passages declare. Then, having done all this firsthand work carefully, we turn to all available helps. We shall read commentaries on these passages. We shall glance at sermons preached by various men on any of these verses or passages. Many facets of thought will shine on us, both from the pages we peruse and from our own minds, the channels of creative thought now being stirred. Finally, we have before us all our exegetical work, our statements of the outstanding ideas, and the result of all our research. We are now ready to begin our direct sermonic work.

Where shall we begin? We begin by further discarding and eliminating. We have found many intriguing ideas in our exegetical study, but these are not our goal. We desire not an exegesis nor exposition, but an expository sermon. We begin therefore with the easiest grade or level for our congregation to reach. We therefore select Luke 11:1-13, with special emphasis on verse 13, "If ye, being evil . . . how much more your Heavenly Father will give . . . ," and compare this with experience and also direct teaching. That is, we have found that mere requests do not always bring the affirmative answer, and also Jesus teaches in Luke 18:1-8 that "Men ought always to pray, and not to faint." We question "Why?" and a suggestion of an answer is given in 18:8, "Nevertheless. . . ." We know that prayer life and faith are consonant. If God demands importunity, or by withholding our petition forces importunity, and if that enforced importunity develops our faith, shall we not be satisfied to continue in prayer, and not faint? We turn to Mark 10:46-52, the story of blind Bartimaeus. Here we have a need at first ignored. Then the spoken prayer is ignored. Finally, when Bartimaeus is so noisy he is disturbing even that oriental crowd, Jesus sends for him. By now the crush is so great that for easier passage he discards his outer garment, presses through the crowd, and after he gets to Jesus, receives his boon. Why not an immediate answer? It may be so that there would be no question as to who did the healing. It may have been to draw a greater crowd. It may even have been to lead Bartimaeus to cast away even that which was of itself good (the robe) so as to "get through"

The Selective Method

to Jesus. (Here we sense a fine opportunity to enforce by illustration, this idea of "getting through." So much prayer gets only to "a wall" and an echo is the answer!)

Now we come to that almost inexplicable story of Matthew 15:21-28. An exegesis has led us to many avenues of thought. There stands out the fact that Jesus did not answer the woman; that he repulsed her, and that she, deep in humiliation, persisted until the granting of her prayer. Why this "begging?" It may have been to teach her the need of deep humility, or it may have been a lesson to the disciples.

Next we consider the story of Moses praying for Israel, Deut. 9:9-26. Why did not God answer the first day, or week? Here is fine opportunity for use of the imagination to illustrate the value of constant prayer in spite of a denial of our plea at the first. Now we turn back to Genesis 18:23-33, a most interesting and yet in some ways a baffling story. Why did not God tell Abraham in the first place that there was only one righteous, Lot, and that he would be saved? Why did God let him beg and torture his soul in the begging, when He knew it was all to no avail? Here again is a fine occasion for the imagination to play, both with the story and its supplication.

Finally we are prepared to record our sermon outline.

Topic: "Why Must Christians Be Beggars?"

Introduction: Deal with Luke 11:13. Inference, "no begging necessary in prayer." Experience proves this untrue. Worthy petitions are not always granted. We do not know why. We venture some surmises which may be in the direction of a satisfactory answer.

I. GOD MAY WANT TO KEEP US PRAYING SO FAITH WILL BE KEPT ALIVE. Luke 18:1-8.
   1. The story, Luke 18:1-8. Too many stop at vs. 7. The "howbeit" is essential.
   2. God plans to answer . . . and is abundantly able.

3. The Christian's prayer-life and faith are vitally related. God knows this, and maybe this is why he makes us keep on praying, even for good things.

II. GOD MAY DESIRE US TO LEARN THE LESSON OF WILLINGNESS TO DISCARD EVEN GOOD THINGS IN ORDER TO GET CLOSE CONTACT WITH HIM. Mark 10:46-52.
  1. The constant praying may or may not gather a crowd. But Satan will at least always be present with a crowd of objections and problems.
  2. God's silence before our needs is not because of ignorance or weakness, but because of some design we cannot now see.
  3. Use an illustration of "praying through." Many conscious of "praying to a wall." Nothing but echo as an answer. Cry of victory, "I know now what you're talking about. I 'got through'." This may come only after soul agony, but how extremely worth-while and unforgettable the experience is!

III. SOME LESSONS IN IMPORTUNATE PRAYER ARE ALMOST INEXPLICABLE. Matt. 15:21-28.
  1. The problems of this story. Silence . . . insult . . . not like Christ!
  2. Let the problem go . . . get the blessing.
  3. Disciples disturbed by her crying . . . finally see the result of her fierce crying and deep humility.
  4. Willingness to grovel . . . beg . . . be a dog . . . to gain the desired end. Reminds us of Paul, willing to be accursed for Israel. Here is the mark of Christ, and a genuine blessing found because of deep and importunate prayer.

IV. IF GOD IS GOING TO ANSWER FAVORABLY IN THE END WHY DOES HE NOT ANSWER SOONER? WHY ALL THE BEGGING AND CRYING? Deut. 9:9-26.
  1. The forty days on Sinai, fasting, with God.
  2. The impatience, the image, the curse. Vs. 14.

3. The broken heart, broken tablets, and retiring to prayer.
4. Forty more days and nights of prayer, with fasting. WHY SO LONG? Use imagination. People outside, angry at first . . . only gradually realize the seriousness of their offense and the depth of Moses' passion for them. When God sees that they are ready, the answer comes.

If God wants us to continue in prayer for no other reason than that others may be readied, shall we not be willing to "pray, and not to faint?"

V. IF GOD IS GOING TO ANSWER UNFAVORABLY IN THE END, AND IT IS POSSIBLE FOR HIM TO MAKE US AWARE OF THE ANSWER, WHY DOES HE NOT SAVE US FROM THE STRESS OF PLEADING? (Genesis 18; 23-33, Abraham pleads for Sodom.)

1. Pleading for the city shows real concern.
2. Bargaining with God is no easy thing . . . picture 50-45-40-30-20-10- . . . real soul-sweat!
3. Having so plead, Abraham MUST HAVE gone to Sodom to reveal his pleading, and the result.
4. In the day of Judgment, Sodom, then, will have no excuse.

If God wants to plead even when the result is predetermined in the negative, so that we shall get so concerned we shall witness and there will then be no excuses at the Judgment . . . shall we not be willing to "pray, and not to faint"?

Conclusion: "He spake this parable unto them, that men ought always to pray and not to faint." He has reasons for insisting on continued prayer; shall we be unwilling to trust Him? Let us "pray, and not faint."

This sermon is on the doctrine of prayer from the practical side. All doctrinal sermons should be practical, even as all "practical" sermons should be deeply doctrinal. To study how the method is applied in other than a doctrinal way we assign the word (or idea) "rod." Our illustration of how this method produces a sermon on this idea is given in Appendix X, page 142.

CHAPTER II

Preaching From Biblical History

Jeff D. Ray emphasizes the difficulty and value of this approach. He says, in his book, *Expository Preaching,* p. 36, "It is one thing to know the facts of history. It is quite another to cause these facts to move before an audience like a living panorama."

One difficulty in the way of explaining this method lies in the fact that the selection of that portion of history which one regards as a unit must be decided in the mind of any given preacher. There are some few portions of Holy Writ which we shall all accept as units. Paul's first missionary journey is one such portion. Whether all would agree in taking all of this — or on the other hand of taking only this — as a unit for sermonic treatment is quite another thing. This selection then is based on subjective factors. One knows the book. He reads it in great sections rather than the impossible "chapter-a-day" or the chaotic "verse-a-day" method. In his reading the preacher concludes that between such an experience and such another experience is a portion which contains and illustrates and emphasizes a certain truth. This selection then is surely arbitrary, although we may well assert it is Spirit-led also.

The first task then is to decide upon the unit, the portion of history which, for the preacher's present purpose, has sermonic value in its entirety and not only in its parts severally. The second step is full familiarity. This familiarity must be so complete that the preacher sees as in a mighty panorama the whole sweep of this history. Seeing it thus in perspective the preacher can now select the several peaks or high spots which stand out strongly. His former decision as to why this portion is a unit will somewhat, if not even quite strongly, cause the preacher to select certain items as high spots and pass over others as rather secondary and tertiary. If his purpose were the teaching of history, he would not have the right thus to select and to discard. His purpose is the preaching of a message based on teaching drawn from a certain period of history and, therefore, he may assume the right thus to do. Having thus selected, the preacher now strives so to re-think his first idea of "theme" as to phrase it in the light of that which is here revealed — or at least the major movement. In the light of this re-thinking (and probably also re-phrasing) he now restudies his material in order both to select and discard, acting now in the light of the demands of his theme. The preacher is usually also a pastor, and the needs of his people will direct him to a considerable extent. This is proper, for he must preach so as to meet their needs.

We take as our first example and illustration of this method a rather familiar story, the travels of Israel, "From Canaan to Canaan." This will cover a long period and much Scripture. From Genesis 37 to Joshua 3, from the selling of Joseph away from Canaan, to "All the people were passed clean over Jordan." An ambitious portion to cover? Difficult to bring down to sermon length? Yes, but this is the expositor's task. There is a truly inspiring lesson here, and the story taken as a whole reveals certain facts more emphatically and clearly than would be the case if the story were taken piecemeal.

We see Israel go down into Egypt in the person of Joseph. We see Israel resident there as a family and go out of Egypt as a tribe and a nation. They went out of Canaan because of a great and sore famine and went back into Canaan to possess "A land flowing with milk and honey." God prepared a nation for its home and the home for its conquerors, that same nation. How can we make just one sermon out of this story? According to the instructions above, we must prepare to discard a tremendous amount of material which, though good, is less than the best as illustrative of the truth we seek to emphasize. That which we finally select will be tabulated carefully, studied and "digested." A more detailed panorama will now be seen. The bright mountain peaks, at first distant, will be now foreground, and that which was incidental foreground will be cleared away. Even these mountain peaks must be scrutinized critically, and some of them set aside as beautiful, but not quite sufficiently relevant to the sermon to be usable.

We seek for vital items. In Genesis we select: chapter 37, the selling of Joseph; 41, Joseph and Pharaoh's dream; 42, Famine; 46-47, Jacob comes to Egypt. We note especially 45:7-8, 49:8-12 and 50:20: the first, "God sent me before you . . . to preserve you . . . so it was not you that sent me hither but God"; the second, "Judah is a lion's whelp . . . the sceptre shall not depart from Judah, nor a lawgiver from between his feet until Shiloh come"; and the third, "Ye thought evil against me but God meant it unto good." Then we turn to Exodus: Here we find new Pharaohs, and persecution. In the second chapter is recorded the birth of Moses, the burning bush in the third, and the fourth, Aaron. In the fifth, the cry, "Let my people go," is heard. Chapters 6-11 tell of the plagues, 12 of the Passover, and 13 of the Exodus. Then in 14 is the story of the crossing of the Red Sea, in 15 the Palms of Elim, in 16, the manna and the quails, in 20 the commandments, in 32 the golden calf (which we compare with Deut. 9:9-26 for the fuller story of Moses' Prayer) and 36-40 the preparing and rearing of the Tabernacle. In Leviticus we find a story of religious rites and ceremonies, in which chapter 16, the Day of Atonement, stands out. In Numbers we find the numbering, the murmuring (which is started by the "mixed multitude") and in chapter 12 the leprosy upon Miriam for seven days because of fomenting rebellion against Moses. Then in chapter 13 we read concerning the spies and the fact that they were sent into Canaan and, returning, report Anakim there. There is rebellion, and God is angry at Israel. Only Caleb and Joshua, of all this people, are to enter the land. Chapter 20:7-13 tells of Moses' disobedience of God in striking angrily at the rock instead of giving glory to God, of God's anger at him, and the punishment — that he is not to enter the promised land, either. In 21 the brazen serpent is pictured and finally in 27:18 Joshua is chosen to be Moses' successor.

Then we read Deuteronomy, which is Moses' Swan Song. We turn to Joshua and read in the first three chapters of the call, challenge, and promise to Joshua, the story of Rahab, and the crossing of the Jordan. Now then, what can we do with even this mass of material save lecture on it and teach the facts of the story?

The story of "From Canaan to Canaan" can be covered by the mention of only seven places! Mamre, Egypt, Red Sea, Sinai, Kadesh-Barnea, Wilderness, Jericho. Or, four names will tell the story: Joseph, Moses, Aaron, Joshua. Or, four facts will suffice to imply the whole; mercy, law, priesthood, victory. In a paragraph the "highlights" of this story can be set forth. A few texts will cause facts to cluster about them; Genesis 45:7-8 and 50:20, Exodus 5, Numbers 13, and Joshua 3. This eliminates much fine material? Yes, but a later and different approach could consider that. To get a lesson from history there must be a far sweep of the mind, both broad and deep. Thus we discover the lessons. The resultant sermon outline, from this story, could well be:

Topic: "From Mamre to Jericho"

Introduction: The Bible is not a history book. Its history is all for a purpose, to reveal God in his dealings with men, and men in their response to those dealings. Therefore we study Bible history, not for the facts, interesting though they are, but to discover God behind those facts. (Here follows a swift bird's-eye view of the story, in about a dozen sentences, built for example on a brief mention of the significance of the seven places above referred to.)

I. IN THIS STORY WE DISCOVER THAT THERE ARE TIMES WHEN EVIL EVENTUATES IN GOOD. (Based on Gen. 45:7-8 and 50-20)

   1. Story of Joseph . . . slave . . . and then master.
   2. The Red Sea . . . a barrier to progress and yet a blessing in protection.

3. Jericho, a strongly walled city, yet an open gate to the promised land.

II. IN THIS STORY WE DISCOVER CERTAIN CAUSES OF EVIL.
  1. In the story of Kadesh Barnea, rebellion against God.
  2. In the story of Miriam, rebellion against God's servant.
  3. In the story of the murmuring, the presence of the "mixed multitude."

III. IN THIS STORY WE DISCOVER CERTAIN CAUSES OF GOOD.
  (Here we might refer to Zech. 4:6, "Not by might nor by power but by my spirit, saith the Lord.")
  1. Joseph is faithful in the midst of trial, and God richly blesses.
  2. Genesis 49:8-12 and Numbers 24:17 . . . "Good" is the intent of God toward all mankind, if man will but receive it.
  3. Leviticus 16, the Day of Atonement . . . God's sure mercies, as here promised and later fulfilled in Christ.

GOOD, then, is a product of GRACE, and given to the faithful. Conclusion. Joshua 1:9, "Have not I commanded thee? Be strong and of a good courage; be not afraid, neither be thou dismayed; for the Lord thy God is with thee whithersoever thou goest."

In order that the student may practice this method we assign for a second portion Judges 21:25 to II Chronicles 36:20. It may be that another person would not select this particular portion; or if he did, the selection might be for a reason different from that in our mind at the present. In order to aid the student at this point then, we call attention to certain factors which caused us to conclude that this was a unit.

The assigned portion begins with, "In those days there was no king in Israel: every man did that which was right in his own eyes." This presents to us a picture of confusion and even chaos. Israel had been a theocracy, assumedly still was a theocracy. The period of the judges had in it certain times of confusion, but the power of the judges was great and the will of God was worked through their God-given wisdom. We come now to a new stage in the history of Israel. In the eighth chapter of I Samuel this prophet is seen as an old man with sons who are not following in his godly ways. There comes the plaint, "Make us a king." In due season the people get their king. The kingdom grows. It almost immediately deteriorates and finally disintegrates. The last verse in the above assigned portion tells of this disintegration and of the captivity. The first verse we repeat, ". . . no king . . . every man did that which was right in his own eyes." The last verses tell us that the priests and the people transgressed, that they "mocked the messengers of God and despised his words" and that the king of the Chaldees "slew their young men," and brought to Babylon "the treasures of the house of the Lord and treasures of the king and his princes." And they burnt the house of God and "them that had escaped from the sword carried he away to Babylon." In view of this we conclude that this is a portion of Scripture which relates the story of "a monarchy that failed," tracing its history from the chaos that preceded that monarchy to the chaos that obtained at its breaking up. It is not thought that the student need retain our theme. We relate it in order that the student may see why the portion chosen was chosen; why it is seen as a unit.

For our illustration of this method used this second time, turn to Appendix XI, page 143.

CHAPTER III

Homiletically Interpreting Events

Very closely related to preaching from history is this method of interpreting the several events within a movement of history, treated as apart from that history, yet of course interpreted in the light of that history. We must understand what we mean by an "event." Paul's first missionary journey, for example, should be treated under the Historical Method, but the separation of Paul from Barnabas over Mark's defection is an event. The Wilderness Wanderings demand the historical treatment, but the Leprosy of Miriam or the Striking of the Rock are events. The difficulty of illustration of this method lies in the fact that we have so many "events" from which to choose, that we are embarrassed by our riches. This method finds great value in the choice of events in whose light we shall develop a series of sermons. This is not to belittle any single sermon on any event, but to suggest the great teaching value if a series is wisely planned. As in other methods, we can but suggest, and each must work out his own final technique in the application of these suggestions.

For an illustration of the use of this technique we turn to the event recorded in Numbers 13:1 to 14:39. This is the very familiar "Kadesh Barnea" experience, and the very familiarity of the experience suggests that it is a "leading" event. This could well be treated as a part of an "historical" treatment, or its characters could be dealt with separately under the biographical method. As an event we neither emphasize the story of which it is a part nor the characters who live in the event. All material, historical or biographical, that lends to an interpretation of the spirit of the event, will of course be "grist to our mill," but will be secondary to our main purpose. In our background study we, of course, review much of the surrounding historical material. We must understand the whole situation and also the characters that brought about the situation. We sense the approach to the place, and the purpose. We read about the spies, their spirit, work and report. We analyze the reception of their report, God's consequent curse upon them, and turning away into the wilderness for forty years until a new people should be raised up. These considerations lead us to entitle our sermon, "The Death Warrant of a People." For introduction we tell the story of the event, swiftly and skilfully sketched so as to bring out the focal points. (We must assume some Bible knowledge on the part of our congregation, but "We must never underestimate the ignorance of church people in Bible History or Doctrine.") We conclude, "The Kadesh Barnea experience was a death warrant for this people."

I. THIS DEATH WARRANT MIGHT WELL HAVE BEEN A BIRTH CERTIFICATE.
   1. God had showed them in the past that he was able to lead them triumphantly.
   2. God promised them his continued leadership, favor and protection.
   3. Had this people followed God, a migrant group of tribes would have been transformed into a stable nation.

II. THIS DEATH WARRANT WAS DEMANDED AND CARRIED OUT NOT BY AN ARBITRARY AND WHIMSICAL GOD, BUT BY THE DELIBERATE ACTS OF THIS PEOPLE.
   1. God permitted the Anakims in the land, but it was the blind fear of the people that enlarged the danger.
   2. God permitted them to choose their own spies, but it was their own fault that they did not choose men of faith and courage.
   3. Had this people acted as God's people, He would have carried them through.

III. THE EXPERIENCE AT KADESH BARNEA, CULMINATING IN THE ISSUANCE OF A DEATH-WARRANT, ALWAYS FOLLOWS THE SAME PROCEDURE.
 1. God manifests His power.
 2. He offers Life to "His own."
 3. Man fails to follow. (Commits SIN)
 4. The wages of sin is DEATH. (Whether for a man or a nation.)

Conclusion: Have you come to this type of place? They . . . go ahead . . . in HIM. And, if and when you do come to this type of experience . . . remember THE DEATH WARRANT OF A PEOPLE, and learn by their failure.

This approach is different from the "historical" only in the length of the portion of Scripture taken for sermonic use. It does have that difference, and therefore is worthy a separate approach. There is another approach which seemingly is very similar. This is dealt with under the title, "Preaching from Geography" (See Part III, chapter 6, page 96.) and compares these three, historical, events, and "places," so as to understand more clearly the difference and various advantages.

For a second study interpreting events we assign "Pentecost." We shall find this a very different sermon, but the process is the same. See Appendix XII, page 146.

A warning note must be sounded at this point. The student will note that in the introduction to this method we stressed the importance of "all material, historical or biographical, that lends to an interpretation of an event" (page 92). Our study of Kadesh-Barnea did not utlize much other historical material than that in the specific passage noted. It is our conviction that Pentecost as an event recorded in Acts 2 cannot be understood apart from the whole history of Pentecost and its meaning to the Jewish people. This "event" was at Pentecost for a reason even as the Last Supper and the Crucifixion were at Passover time.

CHAPTER IV

Preaching From Biblical Biographies

Most people are fascinated by the study of biographies. We are assured, therefore, that if we use biographies as bases for sermons we shall at least have at the start a kind of literature which usually attracts and holds attention. There have been a great many character-studies of Bible people written; so many that we are embarrassed by riches if we go afield searching for material. As true expositors we turn to the Word first in order to discover all that it has to say, turning to the writing and conclusions of other men only after we have unfolded the content of the Word.

Our procedure in this field has five steps. First, we get all of the facts concerning our character, both explicit and implied. Second, we thoroughly study these facts so as to be sure we understand them. We must completely grasp each detail, the relation of each to all others, and severally to all significant surroundings. Third, we analyze the story so as to get a theme for our sermon. We do not desire merely to deliver a lecture on the character in mind, but to bring a certain lesson in a sermon based on that life. Fourth, we arrange the facts in logical order in view of the theme so that the theme correlates all, that progress in evident, and that a properly supported climax is assured. Fifth, in the preaching of this message we are careful to present facts as facts, and yet on the whole present an analytical study with spiritual appeal.

For our first illustration of this method, we study Mark. Our first step is to gather together all material available, every reference to Mark, if it tells us anything about his character, his personality, experience, ideals or background. We may find ourselves driven to use the imagination; and if so, we shall thank God and take heart.

A consecrated imagination is one of the strongest allies of the preacher, and anything that will foster its use and development should be welcomed.

But, to get our facts, few sources are discovered. We find Mark in the Acts, in Colossians, in II Timothy, I Peter and, of course, in his Gospel. We turn to the "Acts." Here, in 12:12, we read of certain experiences which occurred in the home of John Mark in Jerusalem. We find that Peter had been in jail, but was set free by an angel. Then, "When he had considered the thing, he came to the house of Mary, the mother of John, whose surname was Mark, where many had gathered together praying." Then, after the furor of Peter's escape had subsided, and Herod was meanwhile stricken with death from God because of blasphemy, the Word grew and multiplied. We turn to verse 25, "And Barnabas and Saul returned from Jerusalem when they had fulfilled their ministry, and took with them John, whose surname was Mark." Now we read on to Acts 13:5. Here we find the story of Barnabas and Saul being set apart for their work. They departed from Antioch to Seleucia, Cyprus and Salamis, "And they had also John as their attendant." Then we read to verse 13, where we find that after all this, plus travelling to Paphos and the experience with Elymas the sorcerer, the change of Saul's name to Paul, and thence to Perga in Pamphylia, that, "And John, departing from them, returned to Jerusalem."

From this experience of our hero, we turn to Acts 15:37-39. After the completion of the first missionary journey of Paul and Barnabas and the council at Jerusalem, Paul and Barnabas abide in Antioch for some time preaching. These two stalwart souls then proposed to revisit the places in which they witnessed on their first trip. Then: "And Barnabas determined to take with them John, whose surname was Mark. But Paul thought it not good to take him with them, who departed from them at Pamphylia, and went not with them to the work. And the contention was so sharp between them that they parted one from the other; and so Barnabas took Mark and sailed unto Cyprus and Paul chose Silas and departed, being recommended by the brethren unto the grace of God."

Strangely enough, according to Colossians 4:10, we discover that John Mark was with Paul in his first imprisonment. In the same reference we find that Mark was probably nephew to Barnabas, although exegesis leaves a doubt as to the exact relationship. We read, among those who send greetings, "Marcus, sister's son to Barnabas." From Rome Mark evidently went to Babylon with Peter, or at least joined Peter there, for in I Peter 5:13 we read "Marcus my son" sent greetings with Peter from Babylon. And then we find Mark at Ephesus with Timothy, and Paul (strange change!) wrote to him (II Timothy 4:11), "Take Mark and bring him with thee, for he is profitable to me for the ministry."

Our last reference is deliberately left to the last, although chronologically it ought to have come first. There is slight doubt as to whether it does refer to John Mark, but as there is no contrary proof, and there is affirmative argument, we conclude it does so refer. We read in Mark 14:51-52, "And there followed him a certain young man, having a linen cloth about his naked body; and the young men laid hold on him, and he left the linen cloth and fled away from them naked."

Now, what a perfect wealth of fascinating material we have before us, just in the reading of these few passages. Many channels of approach open to us. We think of the boy in what must have been a home of refinement and spirituality. Some critics affirm that the "Upper Room" was in this home. We recall the experience in the Garden, whence Mark fled naked, thus expressing timidity and fear. We follow him back to his home, and to the fellowship with the Apostles and the early Christians in Jerusalem. There occurred wonderful answers to prayer. Mark was given the opportunity to be an "understudy" to Saul and Barnabas, and failed miserably at the task. He ran away again. He was championed later by an affectionate uncle, and his fellowship with Peter was brought about. He was with Timothy, too, and somewhere in the interim had redeemed himself in Paul's sight. Finally, we have the Gospel written, which was quickly accepted by the Christian fellowship, very probably because of its well known Petrine source, yet as definitely by Mark, a worthy scrivener if no more. Now, how shall we preach all this? To teach it is not sufficient. We are preachers, not lecturers; in the pulpit and not rostrum. To inspire and not merely interest or instruct is our task. Yet, as expositors, we may both interest and inspire, teach and preach. After meditation and prayer over our work, with written exegesis and careful condensation before us, we proceed to organize all of our material into a sermon. We sense that in many a soul is the fear of being a coward, with the consciousness that somewhere he has failed. Many sincere hearts are therefore overburdened with a sense of shame for this failure. Our topic, then:

"Mark the Manly"
or
"A Coward's Courage"

Introduction: The scene in the Garden. The coward. But . . . no worse than many others! Many a coward can encourage his heart by the realization that others have the same battles and fears to overcome, and that by no means all succeed! But, Mark finally overcame, and became truly manly.

I. A CHRISTIAN HOME, CHRISTIAN FELLOWSHIP AND EXAMPLES OF CHRISTIAN FORTITUDE DO NOT SUFFICE TO GIVE THE COWARD COURAGE TO CARRY ON IN CHRISTIAN SERVICE. (Here is revealed a mistake in some modern conceptions of religious education, etc.)

1. Mark's home and home life.
2. Peter's release from prison . . . during prayer . . .
3. Mark's chance to understudy Saul and Barnabas.
4. The experiences with Saul and Barnabas.
   (Our coward is still a coward! He has not yet discovered courage.)

II. THE GOSPEL ACCORDING TO MARK IS A PRODUCTION OF A MAN OF COURAGE.

1. Constant use of "straightway."
   (A sense of fearless "rush" to complete the tale.)

2. Unequivocal. 16:16, "He that believeth and is baptized shall be saved, but he that believeth not shall be condemned."
  3. Confesses to own cowardice . . . and that took courage. (14:51-52)
  4. To testify to this redemption of a coward, see Paul's invitation to Timothy, "Bring Mark, for he is profitable to me for the ministry."

III. WHEN DID OUR COWARD GAIN HIS COURAGE?
  1. Early experiences sometimes have more effect in later life than we think. (Godly home a potent influence through the years.)
  2. Christian fellowship is a challenge to the best in a man.
  3. His uncle believed in him.
  4. Peter doubtless told him of his own defection and redemption.

Conclusion: It was a personal relation to and surrender to Jesus Christ, as Peter (and others, of course) revealed Christ to him, that gave him courage.

Are we cowards? Take heart . . . and get close to Christ.

We have thus taught concerning many of the facts of the life of Mark, and we have also presented a sermon. For a further practice on this method, we suggest a study of Thomas. (See Appendix XIII, page 147.) Thomas is widely known in a superficial way. We counsel careful study before the theme of the message is selected.

CHAPTER V

Sermons From Biographies Plus*

We found the Biblical biographies were a great source of sermonic ideas. We now move just a short bit ahead and learn different lessons. These lessons are in part from the lives of these Bible characters but more particularly from their contact with Jesus Christ. It is this contact idea which differentiates this method from the preceding one. In this type of sermon biographical facility is required but the use of a consecrated imagination is much more evident. We shall teach about the character but we add to this the lessons drawn from the way Jesus dealt with that soul. We shall thus incidentally learn about Jesus' way with men. We may even learn something about the art of personal work.

As in the biographical method, it will be essential for us to have a deep, thorough and sympathetic knowledge of each character. We must consider not only every Scripture reference, but as much information about him as we can possibly gather from every source. We must live with him and discover information where casual reading or even ordinary study of the Word will see no reference whatever. Woe unto the expositor who tries to evade responsibility and avoid hard work. There is no end for him but failure.

---

* Surely one would be ungrateful if he did not stop at this point to pay tribute to Dr. G. Campbell Morgan, now of sainted memory. It was my privilege to study at his feet for three years, when he was Professor of New Testament at Gordon College of Theology and Missions, Boston. From the point of view of inspiration and encouragement he was of great help to me in the preparation of this course and this volume. Many ideas could no doubt be traced to his influence and his lectures. This particular chapter presents a method which he used in an entire series of chapel messages at GORDON. I have not knowingly incorporated his words herein, but it is only honest to say that if aught of worth is here, his must be the credit.

Not only must we have this thorough knowledge of our character but also a consecrated and sympathetic knowledge of our Lord. No superficial acquaintance will do. No general knowledge will do. Our information must be specific and in relation to the character at the moment before us. Not until this is complete and exact are we ready to put into sermonic shape what we have learned and dreamed and imagined.

Our introduction will present the character as briefly as possible, withal bringing into that introduction something challenging or interest-provoking. The first sermon division will have to do with the character; the second division will have to do with the contact of Jesus with this character, not so much from an historic point of view, as an interpretative. The third division will be a consideration of the passage for men and women of today, as gleaned from this study. In conclusion we shall present some climax in the experience of this character, and make our appeal from this basis. For example, "The Master of Men Meets Andrew."

For introduction we refer to Andrew as of the very first of the disciples. Call attention to Rev. 21:14, where his name, with the others, is on one of the foundations of the New Jerusalem! We try to arouse interest in "WHY?"

I. THE MAN.
  1. Discernible facts.
    a. Brother of Simon Peter.
    b. Disciple of the Baptist.
    c. Transfers from the Greater (John) to the Greatest (Christ).
    d. First won his brother to Jesus.
    e. Andrew (with Philip) brought the Greeks to Jesus.
    f. It was Andrew who brought the lad with the fishes to Jesus.
  2. Interpretation of these facts.
    a. An unobtrusive man.

      b. A man doing quiet but effective personal work. (He brought Simon ... the lad ... the Greeks ... to Jesus.)
      c. Cautious. (Jesus asked "What seek ye?" He said, "Where dwellest thou?" He wanted time to make enquiry.)
      d. Slow to speak ... deep ... not easily turned ... wholehearted to follow the Truth as he saw it. Loyal, even when his brother became the more prominent.

II. THE METHOD JESUS USED WITH HIM.
    1. Jesus knew why Andrew followed. (John Baptiser had said "Lamb of God.")
    2. Jesus' first words, "What seek ye?" ... not trivial, but heart-searching.
    3. Jesus gave Andrew TIME. ("Abode that day.")
    4. Doubtlessly met the sincere questions of a seeker.
    5. The issue? Jesus gets BOTH Andrew and Simon.

III. THE MESSAGE FOR US.
    1. Jesus knows WHY we come to seek Him out.
    2. He touches the Master-Passion of every life. "What seek ye?"
    3. He will deal with us after our needs ... gives time and thought.
    4. The deep quiet man has a great place in God's work.

Note Acts 2:14 ... Andrew's pleasure as he hears HIS first convert preach this sermon!

Conclusion and appeal: Satisfaction in Christ's work depends not on immediate high position ... but on service, and on long-time results.

In general this will be our procedure, but our sermons will not be monotonously identical for all that. There will be times when a very interesting character will call for more emphasis on the first division. Sometimes Jesus' treatment of that person will be so challenging as to call for greater stress on the second portion. Or, we may desire to dwell more on the lessons for today, and therefore stress the third portion of our sermon. But, beyond this the difference between men, and the difference between the many circumstances in each story, will make a very interest-provoking variety in this type of preaching. For exercise, we assign for a further study using this method, John 4:46-54, The Nobleman. See, for our second example of this method, Appendix XIV, page 149.

CHAPTER VI

Sermons From Geography

For the sake of the contrast and to differentiate as sharply as possible between two similar methods (See Chapter III, "Homiletically Interpreting Events.") we again consider Kadesh Barnea. Our task this time is not merely an interpretation of any one experience at this place, but of the whole history and influence of the place so far as it is revealed in the Bible. This is perhaps a kind of "Historical Method." Our sweep is broad, our preparation therefore a bit hard, but our sermon both interesting and inspiring. A series of sermons on one of the Gospels entitled "With Jesus on the City Streets" would be most profitable. Or, "Through the Years with Moses," or "Mountains Jesus Saw," or "Where Israel Pitched Her Tents." Much pleasure and profit results from this type of study and sermon.

Our first task is to gather together all of the available information concerning the place about which we have elected to preach. This will mean the use of such common resource and research books as will give us such cataloging of places. We shall not slight any reference, but make sure that we have before us every passage of Scripture which either names or refers by implication to this place.

Having tabulated all of this information, the next task is interpretation. We must so deeply "live in" the several passages that we see through and beyond the words on the pages to an understanding of that which occurred there. "The reason why" is fully as important to us as "what."

Our next task might well be called inspiration, for we surely need it, and as surely receive it. We must know how to order all the items of information with the deeper-than-factual knowledge

Sermons From Geography

we have attained. Sermonic development takes place, and we understand how to use this information for the inspiration of our people.

We find eight references to Kadesh. First there is Genesis 14:7, in which verse the place is named in reference to the rebellion of the twelve kings against Chedor-laomer. The rebellion was overthrown. Kadesh is the place of Chedorlaomer's entrance into their territory to sack and plunder them for their rebellion. Numbers 13 and 14 is the locale of our sermon material for the sermon on "Events" (See Chapter III, page 84). The next reference is in Numbers 20:14-21, wherein it is recorded that Kadesh was the place from which Moses sent messengers to the King of Edom, asking for permission to pass through Idumea. This permission was refused. An armed host enforced the refusal, and Israel turned from Kadesh to go toward Mt. Hor. This was really for their own ultimate good. At Mt. Hor, Aaron died, and his son Eleazar was chosen and anointed in his stead. The next reference is in Numbers 27:14. If we compare this with 20:12-14, we discover that Kadesh Barnea was the place where Moses sinned by angrily striking the rock in response to the mumuring of the people. We remind ourselves of the New Testament revelation, "And that Rock was Christ," and determine to bear the inference of this in mind when we come to a study of it. Then come two references which are but passing historical comments, with no added significance (Numbers 32:8, and Deut. 1:19). Now we come to Joshua 10:41 and find Kadesh referred to as the place whence Joshua began one of his forays to conquer the land before him, winning "Because the Lord God of Israel fought for Israel." Now we turn to Joshua 14:7, the last reference. This is again a reference to the experience of Numbers 13 and 14, as recorded in a speech by Joshua. Here he testifies, "And I brought him word again as it was in mine heart," the place of a memorial for a courageous heart!

Now then ... our sermon. Reading these passages over and over, we find that the mention of the place is connected with various experiences. The punishment for rebellion, the spies, the turning back by the Edomites, the Rock and Moses' sin there, the place of opportunity in entering the land ... and finally the place of a memorial to a courageous heart. It so happens that we shall not have to do any eliminating of essential references to the place. We can use them all and strangely enough, nearly in chronological order. Our topic and the final order will naturally depend on our purpose, and of course this will determine how each incident is handled also. That is, we might put the reference to the Rock last, and work out an evangelistic sermon. Or to the turning back by the Edomites, and counsel patience in following God even when things seem untoward. Thus our purpose as well as the demands of the material we shall use, forms the order of development within the sermon.

Topic: "The Transformation of a Memorial"

Introduction: Kadesh Barnea, a memorial place in the Old Testament. Story of Gen. 14:7. These kings remembered it as a place of punishment for rebellion. But, as we see its history we shall find it transformed. And, we shall be amazed at the lessons herein contained for us.

I. THE MEMORIAL OF COWARDLY SPIES AND A FALTERING PEOPLE. Numbers 13 and 14.
   1. The story of the incident.
   2. Ofttimes we carry unpleasant memories of places and failures.

II. THE MEMORIAL OF A HASTY SIN. Numbers 12:12-14.
   1. The story of the incident.
      a. That Rock was Christ. (Cf. I. Cor. 10:4)
      b. Had been stricken once ... now only needed the Voice, in the Name of God.
   2. We remember such haste and sin, and desire to be rid of the memory.

III. THE MEMORIAL OF A FORTUNATE DISAPPOINTMENT. Numbers 20:14-21.

1. The story of the event.
2. Progress is often blocked for our own good.
   (Slight change [H for D] makes Disappointment into His Appointment)
   a. How fortunate that God said "No."

IV. THE MEMORIAL OF A RENEWED OPPORTUNITY. Joshua 10:41.
   1. The story of the event.
   2. It is not true that opportunity knocks but once.
   3. To those who are faithful opportunity is ALWAYS COMING, and under better circumstances than at the first!

Conclusion: Joshua 14:7. The place of cowardly spies and a faltering people was to this man a memorial of a courageous and faithful heart.

Appeal: The EXPERIENCES of others in reference to any place are of no real significance to us. What counts is the attitude of our own hearts to these places and experiences.

Thus we see that a study of one spot or place named in history has a very real value to us, sermonically speaking. Our people may well be greatly blessed by such an approach to the places named in history.

For a second study utilizing this method we suggest the use of "Bethany." Our conclusions as result of this second study will be found in Appendix XV, page 151.

Part IV

PREACHING FROM VARIOUS SPECIFIC KINDS OF LITERATURE

Introduction to Part IV

This Part could be lengthened into several volumes. Our effort in this present volume has been specific and practical. The size of the volume is somewhat limited by various factors, perhaps the most powerful one being it was planned as a textbook for a one-semester course and could not therefore be other than introductory.

However, we do include a study into ways of handling four kinds of Biblical literature. "Parables" and "Prayer" perhaps could have been included in Part II, and handled by the "exegetical-expository" or "paragraphing" method. The Psalter is assuredly worthy of one or more volumes. Prophetic and apocalyptic literature we have treated in generalities only.

Why then a separate division? Largely in order that the reader may be aware that, having reached this stage of study he has only been introduced to the ways in which he may "preach the Word;" that he will feel a sense of incompleteness in reference to the work this volume presents; and that he will embark on a voyage of discovery — going now "on his own steam." Hence, Part IV!

CHAPTER I

Preaching on Parables

Many studies in the parables are available. The number of books of sermonic or exegetical studies based on them is legion. Obviously there is great ground for variety of approach in this realm, and without question we shall always be ready to start anew in our studies in this field. The beauty of this method is that it is perennially fresh, as fresh as homely and practical.

But, though there is such variety of approach, there are nevertheless certain factors of interpretation which we must know in order that we may make the clearest interpretation.

We must be cognizant of the fact that at a definite period in Jesus' ministry he resolutely turned to the use of parables (Mark 4:33-34 and Matt. 13:34). It is most interesting to note that just at this point in His ministry he met a great and growing hostility. Jesus did not seek to hide His message because of this hostility. He desired to draw men on to search for eternal verities that He had come to proclaim. It is true that in many of the parables there seems to be a veiled truth. Jesus said (Matt. 13:53) after the disciples averred that they had understood him, "Every scribe who is instructed unto the Kingdom of Heaven is like unto a man that is an householder, which bringeth forth out of his treasure things new and old." We compare this with verse 35, "That it might be fulfilled which was spoken by the prophet saying, 'I will utter things which have been kept secret from the foundation of the world'" (Ps. 78:2-3). If then the truth was in any sense veiled, it was so veiled as to intrigue men to search out its inner meaning, sufficiently veiled only to intrigue and not to balk them in their search. But there is another aspect to this problem. Who can doubt that Jesus knew He was speaking for the twentieth century as well as for the first? Or at least knew that, being Divine, His words would thus apply? The Eternal Christ speaks Eternal Words. We may then expect that His parables, as indeed also His other teachings, will be not only applicable to our modern life but will also in places, even at this day, reveal things which have been "kept secret from the foundation of the world." This then is the purpose of these parables.

There are definite rules of interpretation. We must remember that these are parables. They are not fables or history or prophecy. They may bear resemblance to fables, or contain history, or be prophetic. But, they are parables; that is, stories whose main line or lines of thought will lie alongside of the truths illustrated or revealed or emphasized. We must search out the subject, for usually there is only one. We must seek for life and not dogma, yet all the while remembering that Jesus' parables must have been based on probabilities of dogmas, and certainly none would be couched in terms contrary to truth or probability. That is, while we may not build a dogma around a parable, surely Christ's dogmas and parables must not disagree. We must interpret the parables in keeping with the whole tone and spirit and procession of His message. This is not a mere teacher who speaks, but the Eternal Christ. We must seek present practical application and illustration of these eternal truths. Simplicity and naturalness are the twin keys to unlock these truths. Anything forced or involved may instantly be suspected as being foreign to the genius of the parable.

There are two kinds of parables: the complete parable and the parabolic illustration. The latter, if used as sermonic material, is better classed under the microscopic method; hence we take no note of it here beyond this mention. For our illustration we turn to a complete parable Matthew 20:1-16. If this outline is compared with the illustration of the spiritualizing method (q.v.) where the same passage is employed, the difference will readily be seen. This comparison will, of course, also serve to intensify what we have already said, that some passages lend themselves to treatment under several methods, each with equal correctness, and that the method to be decided upon is not reached by rule or rote, but arbitrarily, according to the mind of the preacher and the needs of the people as he sees them, while other passages seem to be amenable only to one type of method. This same factor is discovered in the study of textual preaching.

In accordance with our rules of interpretation we have three particular things to do with this parable: (1) discover the subject, (2) explain the figures, (3) apply the lesson. This is not always the sermonic procedure in just so many words, but in general it covers the steps of preparation. Other topics may seem better for publicity, but we simply put down, "The Parable of the Vineyard and the Laborers."

Introduction: Discover the subject. Compare 19:30, "But," and 20:1, "So." Refer to 19:16-22, the story of the rich young ruler . . . Peter's question, vs. 27, as to their rewards. Problem then treats not of salvation, but of service and rewards. (Topic ought to aim toward this theme, if not name it.)

I. THE FIGURES USED.

1. The householder . . . vineyard . . . laborers needed.
2. Hands needed for labor.
3. Each man called . . . and each went in answer to a definite call.
4. As the day advances, more are hired.
   The first have a fixed scale . . . the rest, "What is just."
5. Pay-time comes at the close of the day.
   Last hired, first paid . . . each paid the same . . . the first-hired murmur.
6. The answer to the murmuring . . . Generosity is no just ground for complaint as long as justice has already been done.

II. THE LESSON OF THE PARABLE.
1. Payment which is just will be accorded to all.
2. Payment not on basis of long service or of quantity of work done.
3. Payment is purely on the basis of fidelity to opportunity.
4. Here is a suggestion of a deeper reward.
   Those last hired, feeling grateful, are rewarded in their own sense of appreciation, while the others lose part of their reward in their grumbling.

Lesson: Be faithful to your opportunities. God will reward justly. . . . Not work done or years in service, but FAITHFULNESS TO OPPORTUNITY is the basis for reward.

A second parable, Luke 10:25-37 is assigned for study, using this method. Our findings after this study are recorded in Appendix XVI, page 153.

CHAPTER II

Preaching on Prayers

For every different type of literature within the covers of our Bible there is naturally a different method of approach. This method is not so much concerned directly with promoting a prayer life, but rather with preaching expository sermons based on prayers. Of course we desire to promote a warm prayer-life on the part of Christians. We shall discover that this method will help to that end.

Our first task is to discover prayers. In our study to discover prayers, we shall find that we frequently have the opportunity to teach concerning what is or what is not prayer, and what is acceptable, and many other factors in reference to "The Christian's Vital Breath." We shall discover, and of course teach, that prayers are not formal, nor do the words spoken or unspoken prove whether or not we have a prayer before us. We shall discover, to ourselves and the congregation, that the vital element in prayer is not petition nor intercession nor praise, but communion . . . an interchange of mind with Mind. And of course we shall see that it is always essential that man shall approach God. Many conversations between God and His children are recorded for us, but there is no prayer evident. Sometimes in the midst of such conversation we find a short prayer, poignant in its appeal and extremely valuable as the theme for a sermon. In this case, of course, we ordinarily shall use the microscopic approach, though we may decide on another method for purposes of our own. We shall find, and declare, that the answers are always reasonable, whether affirmative or negative, and we shall find that the practice of prayer is practicable and that to be of value it must be constant. These remarks may not have to do with method directly, yet they do emphasize what expository sermons on prayers will enable us to teach.

In the main there will be three portions to these sermons. We shall have the didactic portion, in which we introduce the character and the conditions that call forth this particular prayer. Some exegesis may come into this, but it will be primarily didactic. Then will come the portion mainly exegetical, in which we shall interpret the elements of the prayer, phrases, words and so forth. Finally we shall come to the portion mainly hortatory, in which we shall descant upon the lessons, for us: in the background, subject matter, exegesis, or any other phase desired. We shall, of course, find that a consecrated imagination not only will lend value to this type of approach, but also that it is essential. We must "think ourselves into the situation" so as to interpret correctly not only its material but its spirit and intent. For example we study the prayer of Adam, which in words is scarcely a prayer. Our Scripture portion is Genesis 3:1-21. We deliberately take this passage so as to illustrate deep values, as, for example, revealed in the second sentence of our introduction.

Topic: "Adam's Prayer"

Introduction: Wide latitude needed to discover real prayers. Words not essential, the spirit is what counts. Value in studying the prayers of men and women who, like us, failed, and sought "A Way Back."

I. THE MAN WHO PRAYED. Adam.

    1. No inherited tendencies to evil.

    2. Environment satisfactory.

    3. Unspeakably great blessings granted.

    4. Carefully warned of dangers ahead.

    5. Listened to the voice of the tempter.

II. THE CONDITIONS THAT CALLED FORTH THE PRAYER.
1. Lack of experiential confidence in God.
2. Willingness to seek self-preferment.
3. Conscious of evil . . . when it was too late.
4. Afraid to meet God, and the consequences of his own sin.
5. Tried to pass on responsibility to others.

III. THE ESSENTIAL FACTORS OF THIS PRAYER.
1. Admits knowledge of the reality of God.
2. Admits a wholesome fear of God.
3. Admits, by inference, the justice of the results of his own sin.
4. Tries to offer excuses for his failure.
5. No suggestion of repentance.

IV. THE RESULTS OF THIS PRAYER.
(The prayer contains no petition.)
1. The inevitable results of sin are felt.
2. The unspoken request is granted . . . vs. 15 (cf. Job . . . Daysman).

Conclusion: Lessons to us.

1. Temptation has many sources (good heredity and environment no safeguard).

2. We cannot dodge responsibility.

3. Knowledge about and admission of the fact of . . . and even wholesome fear of God, is no guarantee of safety.

4. God cares and provides a way of security, even though punishment for sin is inevitable.

We thank God for our "Daysman."

For a second study using this method we assign Genesis 4:1-15. We warn the student that it is not an easy passage. As in the use of the passage selected for this first example, we have deliberately assigned a difficult passage in order that the student may have his imagination tested and used along with his exegetical acumen. For example, see Appendix XVII, page 155.

CHAPTER III

Preaching From the Psalms

The Psalm book is a particular kind of Biblical literature. According to the concept of the Jewish world it is as fully inspired (God-in-breathed) as any other of the Old Testament writings; but it is not regarded as being of as much authority as are the Law or the Prophets. When we preach from the Psalms therefore, we ought to realize that we are using a book of "writings," quite different from the other Hebrew religious scrolls. Surely these words are "Scripture." They are replete with history and prophecy, and yet are not susceptible of the same treatment as either historical or prophetical literature. Neither are they mere poesy!

The Psalter is full of nourishment for our lives and hearts. Jesus must have spent a great amount of time reading the Psalter, for he quotes it copiously. All moods of life are here, whether of joy or grief. This is a human book with Divine compassion. How can we best unfold these values before our people? They desire not a technical study of the details which exegesis will reveal, but a life guiding message which spiritual insight will discover.

> "The Psalter in its portrayal of the movement of spiritual experience of the people of God has imperishable value. If we allow the Psalter to speak to us, it will speak the word of God and address itself to our modern world. It has searched the deeps of Deity and speaks with authority in matters theological; it has felt the throbbing pulse beat of mankind; sin and depravity, forgiveness and renewal, death and the life beyond; it will find us in its analysis and point to us the way of life; it has divined the coming Messiah: his humanity, his

sufferings, his kingly glory — did not our Lord point out in all the Psalms the things concerning himself? In short, it is our hymn book for this pilgrimage journey, encouraging us in all the vicissitudes of life, teaching our lisping tongues Immanuel's praises and by his encouragement and instruction, causes us to triumph so that by the Lord we can run through a troop of problems and climb unsurmountable difficulties."[1]

We must learn to appreciate the Psalms as such. If ours has been mostly the technical and exegetical approach, with perhaps a goodly emphasis on carefully historical investigation, probably we shall not readily get the greatest value out of the Psalms. And even within the Psalter there are various types of literature: such as praise, confidence, imprecation, Messianic, deliverance, etc., so that our problem is made yet greater than it seemed at the first.

One ought first perhaps decide what type of spirit is appropriate for the occasion in mind, and then to elect a Psalm in harmony with this need. (Obviously this demands a very good acquaintance with the Psalter!) One doubtless will want to read other Psalms in the same category partly for reference and exegesis but partly just to grasp the swing and movement of that literature.

One must read the Psalms over and over again until a title stands forth. This is a much better procedure than that of borrowing the title another has affixed to it. One must note all quotations within the Psalm from other Scripture and also discover how the Psalm is itself quoted. For example, Psalm 144 is made up of a mosaic from Psalms 18, 8, 104, and 33. Psalms 95 is freely quoted in Hebrews 3 and 4. For our first study in this method we shall use this latter Psalm, temporarily entitling it:

"Treading His Courts with Fear"

We read it so many times that its several parts or "movements" stand clearly before us. These parts are 1-7a, 7b-11. First the Levitical choir is to sing, probably as the people enter the temple for worship. The exhortation to sing is in vss. 1-2. Then the reason

---

[1]. Prof. E. R. Dalglish, one time Prof. of O.T., Gordon Divinity School, Beverly Farms, Mass. (an unpublished MS.).

for this exhortation is given in vss. 3-5. Then ascends another Psalm in vss. 6-7a. Then the Psalmist has the choir or perhaps a priest cry out, vs. 7b, "Today, oh, that ye would hear his voice. . . ." After that, as a part of this cry, is the illustration of when Israel did harden her heart and what happened to her as a result.

Now then, having thus grasped the heart of the Psalm and expressed it in a topic, and then having discovered the outline or movement of the Psalm — what shall we do with it sermonically? Let us finally entitle it,

"Singing, Yet with Fear"

I. LET US SING. Vss. 1-2 and 6-7a.
   (Note for exegetical study: — use all allusions and every idea which is contained.)
   1. Singing is not a matter of notes and harmony in music, but of the attitude of the soul.
   2. All praise is due to Jesus Christ our Lord (The Rock).
   3. Self-forgetful humility is essential in worship (bowing down).

II. LET US EXALT. Vss. 3-5.
   1. Our Lord is God.
   2. All creation is His and we also. (cf. 7a)

III. LET US IN FEAR HAVE FAITH. Vss. 7b-11.
   1. Brazen affrontery could result if we test and tempt our God. (as at "Meribah and Massah." See Ex. 17:1-7.)
   2. Error in the heart is basic cause of much mischief.
   3. Knowing His ways cannot follow from ignorance of the glory of His Person.

Conclusion: We have sung and do sing. This is good, but let us be warned lest we be of those who have His Name and yet do not "Enter into His rest." Vs. 11 (cf. Deut. 12:9-10).

For a second study of this method in preaching we suggest the use of Psalm 19. Our conclusions on this portion will be found in Appendix XVIII, page 156.

IV

Preaching from Prophetic and Apocalyptic Literature

Prophetic and apocalyptic Biblical literature was not in our purview in the planning of this course, nor is it our plan to present such studies in detail. Students have consistently raised questions concerning this matter, hence our decision to include this brief chapter in our study.

Fully to study the possible ways of preaching from this literature demands a separate book and course. We once taught such a course, using the Revelation for our material. This was a rewarding study, but obviously is too big to be included in this text. History must be understood to perfection. Cross-references in the Bible must be assiduously studied and compared. The science of hermeneutics must be brought into full play. Pre-dispositions ordinarily should play no part, but unfortunately here they must for we cannot study this literature for homiletical purposes without first studying it for itself. This involves searching out and accepting certain conclusions in reference to dates, to determine what of the far past was prophetic of the nearer past, what of prophetic writing was actually foretelling and what of foretelling is still future. We take the typical conservative view, very moderately dispensational, definitely premillennial. Our study of these various portions of the Bible would naturally be guided by that predetermined view and would be enthusiastic in vindication of prophecy and emphatic in sure hope of premillennial eschatology.

Referring particularly to the writings of the prophets we may assuredly say that they are not "past, ancient, and dead," neither are they primarily "future." There is an absolute timeliness about these writings, yet also a timelessness. They are living and have to do with life. Many of the conditions surrounding these authors are different, one from the other, and yet in the large, they are similar. These are: God, man, sin, intrigue, etc., etc. — pretty much the same in all of these books.

The prophets have a message for our day as well as a record of a past day and a revelation of a day to come. It is our task to discover from the writings of these men of so long ago — these timely and timeless writings — a message for our own day and age.

There are certain general principles which can be stressed and utilized whatever one's predisposition as to eschatology. These principles will help one to preach from the prophetic and apocalyptic literature. It may be that these principles veer into the realm of hermeneutic, but that cannot be helped.

Our first principle is that the Bible is God's Word inscripturated. In its autographa it is completely true as to historic statement, moral precepts and spiritual revelation. It is our task then to discover what the autographs actually said.

Our second principle is that the dates of the several books of the Bible are quite well established. For a long time higher criticism affirmed very late dates for certain portions (mostly to avoid prophecy!) but every discovery that has any bearing on this matter has strengthened our faith in the earlier dates.

Our third principle, which grows out of the first two, is that therefore, the Bible, if and when really known in its entirety both in broad panoramic scenes and in its minutest detail, is its own best supporter and interpreter.

Our fourth principle is to avoid all overstress on the foretelling and strive to present all that is history as history. There is still plenty of foretelling left, and we shall not be overtaken by the danger of becoming fanatical or even grotesque in our interpretation.

Our fifth principle is that, whereas most prophecy of very old time was not susceptible of dating as to fulfillment, and its fulfillment is seen only as later Scripture declares that such an event or condition is the fulfillment of such a prophecy, we should neither strive to date that which we consider as yet future, nor apply

Preaching From Prophetic and Apocapolytic Literature 123

Bible prophecies to events in our immediate time. Too many have been proved unwise because yet more events have revealed such "fulfillment" as not such at all.

Our sixth principle is that it is the part of wisdom for mere man to say concerning the as-yet-unfulfilled prophecies of Holy Writ — "I do not know." We can be sure that such prophecies as have been fulfilled have been fulfilled to amazingly minute detail. This being so, we are right in assuming that remaining prophecies will be fulfilled in like manner. Beyond this we cannot go.

Our seventh principle is that we ought to "speak that we do know and testify that we have seen." There is enough in the Bible of precepts variously revealed, of doctrines severally made clear, of indisputable revelations of God's sure word which we can understand, that we shall profitably spend a lifetime in this literature and never cover all the truth available to us.

Our eighth principle is that the expositor is insatiable. He is not willing to let any Scripture lie for long unstudied, so he will constantly study and search and compare, bringing out of his treasures, "things both new and old."

God will abundantly reward such search. Our horizon will constantly widen, but humility will always grace our pronouncement.

Conclusion

Now we have concluded our dissertation. That we have completely covered the theme we do not assert, for so long as there are minds that will "search the Scriptures," so long there will be differing ideas, and new light on the methods of setting forth that which that search discloses.

It may seem that some of the methods we have been setting forth are forced or impressionistic. There are perhaps several ways out of this dilemma for the expositor. One is to try a composite method, as different phases of the passage may demand different treatment. But better yet is the other way . . . evolve or discover a new method! When the earlier stages of this book were emerging, we, as is stated in the introduction, searched in vain for much helpful material as to methods. Five books were the sum total of our discovery. Now, let every expository preacher add to this report his own well-studied conclusions. Let this book be the priming for the pump of each one's study, and this author's work will be well rewarded.

One thing is sure: this type of preaching, if faithfully prosecuted, will give one a veritable reservoir of preachable texts and passages . . . a reservoir at whose bottom there will be a great spring. The expositor will then frequently find that he is preaching out of the "overflow." Not the overflow of material and temporal substance or experience, but of the Word, for it will well up within him and pour out a clear stream, enriching all to whom such a one ministers.

As we conclude, we set forth afresh the same phrase that started all this search, but with, we hope, a clearer understanding of "How" than we formerly had:

"PREACH THE WORD."

APPENDICES

Introduction to Appendices

The second illustration of each method presented in the basic part of this text, is herein given. It is urged upon the student that he not review the second illustration in this appendix until he has completed his own original work on the assigned passage. Comparison should then be made, not for the purpose of discovering comparative homiletic (or even exegetical!) values, but solely on the basis of understanding of method.

Appendix I

Second illustration of the Exegetical-Expository method, based on the assigned text, Mark 2:13-3:6.

This passage is entirely different from the first one, both as to spirit and purpose, yet it lends itself very readily to the exegetical-expository method.

Our first approach is the same as in the preceding study. Our list of words and verses; our page of egetical material and finally our page of rough outline is along the same manner of procedure as before. Then we "polish" the outline, and get the following result.

Topic: "The Joys of Jesus" (Or, The Calmness of the Christ)

Introduction: The spirit of this whole section is in reference to the undisturbable calm of the Christ in the face of violent criticism. Because we all desire calm spirits, a study of Him at this time ought to be of value to us all.

I. THE UNDISTURBABLE CALM OF THE CHRIST IN THE FACE OF CRITICISM IN REGARD TO THE OVERTURNING OF ANCIENT TRADITIONS CONCERNING SOCIAL CUSTOMS, THE RECOGNITION OF CLASS AND CAST SHOULD ILLUSTRATE TO US OUR NEED IN LIKE SITUATIONS. 2: 15-17.

   1. The criticisms of the Pharisees. Vs. 16.
       Publicans and sinners?

   2. The answer of Jesus. Vs. 17a. (Sick . . .?) (Same word, *Kakos*, translated "evil" in 9:39, Rom. 7:19 and 12:17, etc. etc.)

3. The revealing of a great purpose. Vs. 17b. (This word, "sinners," *hamartoulous*, meaning "those that are missing the mark" i.e., A sufficiently great purpose allows no lesser obstructions.)

II. THE UNDISTURBABLE CALM OF THE CHRIST IN THE FACE OF CRITICISMS REGARDING THE UPSETTING OF RELIGIOUS CUSTOMS OUGHT TO BE OF GUIDANCE TO US. (To fasting, etc.) 2:18-22.
   1. The custom. Vs. 18. (Suggested translation, "And there were the disciples of John . . . engaged in fasting" i.e., right then.)
   2. The answer. Vs. 19. (Purposeless fasting always useless.)
   3. The prophecy. Vs. 20. (*en ekeine te hemera*, "that day," or "those days")
   4. Parable of illustration. Vss. 21-22.
      a. Christ came to impart a new life and way. Cannot be patched onto the old.
      b. He reveals a new life-principle, which old forms cannot express.
      c. He did not rejoice to upset the old, but to establish the new.

III. THE UNDISTURBABLE CALM OF THE CHRIST IN THE FACE OF CRITICISM IN REGARD TO THE OVERTURNING OF ANCIENT SABBATH TRADITIONS OUGHT TO BE OF GUIDANCE TO US. 2:23-3:5.
   1. The sanctity of the Jewish Sabbath.
   2. Many of the externals of sanctification taught by the Talmuds, and the Pharisaic interpretations of these laws.
   3. Jesus and His disciples broke these traditions, both in the Temple and in the cornfield.
      a. Did they winnow the odd handful of wheat-ears and incidentally eat, or pluck the ears so as to "build a path"?

b. Did they do something unallowable on the Sabbath, or did they, on the Sabbath, do something unallowable? David, of necessity, did something otherwise unallowable.
4. Jesus' answer to His critics.
   a. Their traditions not well founded. Vss. 25-26.
   b. They have not understood the purpose of the original law. Vs. 27.
   c. "Therefore" . . . not in a causative sense, but like a transitive verb, subject acted upon . . . action reflexive . . . . "The Son of man is Lord" BECAUSE the Sabbath was made for man and not vice versa. (He is Lord not only over primary things, but also over subsidiary things.) Vss. 28 3:1-5. Emphatic repetition of former teachings.

Conclusion: Note 3:6. The presence and work of Christ may make evil forces unite; i.e., His very calm action and demeanor makes them to quake and take protective steps. Union may be proof of demoniacal activity, and not of Divine Blessing.

The calm of the Christ was not occasioned by the power to do the things He did. He had an inner and unquenchable joy that swept aside all criticisms of Him and His work. He knew He was here to do a greater thing, and nothing smaller than His goal and no authority less than God could deter Him.

Criticism disturbs and stops those who have a lesser command and a wavering faith in the value of their goal.

Let us learn from the Christ how to be calm and serene and full of joy.

Appendix II

Our second illustration of the microscopic expository sermon is based on the "World's Little Bible," John 3:16. This is admittedly a difficult text from which to preach, but the attempt is accompanied with blessings.

Topic: "The World's Little Bible"

Introduction: This phrase used of John 3:16. Magnitude of the text, showing masterly control of language and revelation challenges us just sufficiently to enlarge upon it so as to interpret it to our age!

I. A PROPOSITION IS DECLARED. "For God so loved the world."
   1. "For" . . . a connective . . . looks back on "As Moses lifted the Serpent," and forward to "So also must the Son be lifted." Our text explains what made the lifting of the serpent valuable, and also what made the lifting of the Son possible. LOVE is the secret of the law, as well as the fulfilling thereof. (Cf. Num. 21).
   2. "GOD" . . . Reality! Personality! Vitality!
   3. "SO LOVED."
      a. "So" — *outos* — declarative — "In this manner."
      b. Infinite love not amenable to finite definition.
      c. Manifestation was the only way.
   4. "The world." Not the *things* of the world . . . but the whole of that which He ordered and systematized.
      a. *Ton kosmon* — "the cosmos."
      b. Not the Jews only, nor the Aryans, nor the Wise . . . but ALL THE WORLD.
      c. As to the peoples of the cosmos.

II. A RESULTANT ACTION IS PRESENTED FOR OUR CONSIDERATION. "That He gave His only begotten Son."
   1. Magnitude of Divine Love seen in the magnitude of the Divine Gift.
   2. If all humans were divine, and the difference were of degree only, why "only begotten"?
   3. "SON" . . . Title of office, and no time-inference here.

III. A VERY DEFINITE PURPOSE IS REVEALED "That whosoever believeth on Him might not perish but have eternal life."

1. "That" ... *ina* ... in order that (There was no other way.).
2. "Whosoever" ... Universality of willingness.
3. "Believeth on Him" ... (*Eis* ... "into" ...)
4. "HAVE" ... Now ... "Not perish, but HAVE eternal life." "Eternal," then not continuation ad infinitum that which now is, but refers to a quality of life. Never ending (*aionion*) to be sure, but this is but incidental. "This is life eternal, that they might know Thee, the only true God, and Jesus Christ whom Thou hast sent." This quality of life which Jesus came to give ... like His ... therefore ... "Never die."

Conclusion: "Might not perish" (*apoletai* — used of the destruction and punishment of sinners in another life.) Matt. 10:28, 18:14, Rom. 2:12, etc. ... Possibility? No, a surety — without this way out! Let us walk in this way NOW!

Appendix III

A second illustration of the "Paragraphing Method" is taken from Matthew 21:1-11. We do not give all of the details of the outline, but merely suggest it to the student.

Topic: "Who Is This?"

Introduction: The occasion of the question, and the modern sound of it. The passage suggests.

I. THE LOWLY ONE (Taken from vs. 7).
1. Borrowed beast.
2. Borrowed clothes.
3. Helped to His humble seat.

II. THE SON OF DAVID (Taken from vs. 9).
   1. Blessed is he . . . in the Name.
   2. Thy King (Humanly in the kingly line).

III. THE KING OF ZION (Taken from vs. 5).
   1. Zion — Jerusalem.
   2. Thy King — as above, historical lineage.
   3. Yet, spiritualize, eternal King of Eternal City.

IV. THE LORD (Taken from vs. 3).
   1. Foreknowledge.
   2. "Hath need" (!)
   3. Humans must answer the Lord's needs as He works with and for humans.

Conclusion: "The touch of His hand on mine" . . . When, by personal experience, we make this One really our own, then and then alone can we really know Him. Language fails to explain the greatest and deepest things. So here. Must know by experience in order to find out who He really is.

The above outline will reveal the principle that the verses or groups of verses need not be in any special order. The progression of the sermon to a desired goal is far more important than the arrangement of the verses.

Appendix IV

Our second illustration of "Spiritualizing by Diverting," based on Matthew 15:1-20, is here recorded.

Topic: "On Keeping Clean"

Introduction: Hypocrites are always in trouble, and are always making trouble.

I. THE REAL PROBLEM OF CLEANLINESS RELATES NOT SO MUCH TO THE MORAL LAW BUT TO TRADITIONS THAT HAVE COME TO SURROUND IT.
   1. The very traditions themselves may be in transgression of the Moral Law.
   2. God's Word transcends the ingenious phrasing of what "seems to be right."
   3. Lip service without corresponding spirit is utterly vain.
   4. If we note the law, and disregard the tradition, we shall have no problems here.

II. THE SOURCES OF DEFILEMENT ARE WITHIN AND NOT WITHOUT.
   1. Cf. vss. 11 and 19 . . . "Out of the heart" . . . "As a man thinketh in his heart."
   2. Externalities of tradition or ceremony are utterly unrelated to defilement.

III. WHAT SHOULD OUR ATTITUDE BE TOWARD OUR CRITICS?
   1. Hypocrites are always offended at the truth.
   2. They are not our responsibility. We must not cast our pearls before swine.

Conclusion:

a. Disregard external observances insofar as they claim to be absolute in relation to cleanness or defilement.

b. Regard well the body, for "Ye are the temples of the Holy Spirit."

c. Give primary consideration to the condition of the heart. While that which man sees may be an important index to what is within, God judges on the basis of what is truly within. Ceremony has its place, but is not important to produce or hinder true righteousness.

Appendix V

For the second illustration of "Spiritualizing by Illustrating Life by an Apt Text" we record the results of our study of the second chapter of the "Lamentations."

Topic: "Sorrow's Goal"

Introduction: The first chapter gave us opportunity to call attention to the Prophet, who with bleeding heart saw the desolation of Jerusalem which he had prophesied. Today we discover in this second stanza of this dirge, the goal of that sorrow.

I. THE GOAL OF SORROW AS TAUGHT TO ISRAEL IN THE SECOND STANZA OF THIS DIRGE.
   1. What God hath done. Vss. 1-9.
      a. Anger . . . no pity . . . swallowed up . . . burned against Jacob like a fire . . . stood with his right as an adversary . . . He hath violently taken away His tabernacle . . . He hath cast off His altar.
      b. The result of this action.
         Her gates and bars gone.
         Her king and princes with the Gentiles.
         No more law.
         Her prophets find no more vision [cf. Prov. 29:18, "Where there is no vision, the people perish (cast off restraint)."]
   2. What have the people done about it? Vss. 10-12.
      a. Mournful and hopeless silence of the leaders (elders). Vs. 10a.
      b. Shamed silence of organized religion (virgins). Vs. 10b.
      c. The distress of youth over the conditions. Vss. 11-12.
   3. The cause of these terrible conditions? Vss. 13-17.
      "False prophets." Vs. 14.

4. What does the prophet advise now? Vss. 18-19.
      Ceaseless crying and prayer before Jehovah.
II. THE GOAL OF SORROW FOR OUR DAY AS TAUGHT IN THIS STANZA.
   1. These are terrible days for all nations and people.
   2. God hath not yet fully shown us His anger . . . How blessed the restraint of God, and His patience! (See II Thes. 2:7, "The mystery of iniquity doth already work, only he that letteth will let until he be taken out of the way.")
   3. Yet, much the same results are seen as in the day of Jeremiah. Gates down . . . leaders scattered . . . no law . . . NO VISION.
   4. What has been done? PRACTICALLY NOTHING.
      a. Mournful helplessness of the leaders (elders).
      b. Shamed silence of the churches.
      c. Distress of youth over the conditions.
   5. What is the cause? THE SAME . . . FALSE PROPHETS!
   6. What ought to be done? CEASELESS CRYING AND PRAYER TO JEHOVAH. "Men ought always to pray and not to faint." "Arise, cry out in the night . . . Pour out thy heart like water." "Watch and pray for ye know not the hour." The turn of thought seems to imply — "no affirmative answer." Let not vs. 22 be found true here!!!! Let our sorrow provoke prayer, which is its real goal. GODLY SORROW WORKETH REPENTANCE.

Appendix VI

Our second illustration of using "Portraiture as a Backdrop for Exposition" is also taken from the Revelation. It is not to be thought that this is the way to preach this whole book, nor indeed, as we have already cautioned, is it to be thought that this is the only way to preach these portions of the book. These illustrations are to be taken for just that and nothing more. The picture in chapter four we entitle, "Through the Gate of Glory."

For introduction we "place" the chapter. In this, of course, we teach concerning the exegesis of the book. Chapter one reveals Christ and His place in relation to His Church. Chapters two and three are His messages to the Church. Here, in chapter four, we have a pictorial interlude, the Throne. In five we have the book, six, the opening of six of the seals of that book. Seven is another interlude. Eight is the breaking of the seventh seal, and the beginning of the end. Nine and ten go clear to the "end of time" (cf. 10:17). Eleven through eighteen tell of the last judgment, nineteen and twenty of the triumph, and twenty-one and twenty-two of the New Jerusalem. This is a rather bold outline but it places our chapter in the scheme of the book. "I want to tell you of a glimpse into the future which my Lord gave me . . . but first let me tell you of the Throne I saw," says John.

Note 1 and 2a. John was brought out of the earth into the spirit realm. He saw a picture beyond description by the human tongue, yet he does his best. Let us look at that picture, too.

I. BEHOLD! A THRONE!

   1. The One on the throne.
Like Jasper and Sardius. (cf. Ex. 28:17-20.) The jewels on the breastplate of the high priest, the first mentioned is the jasper and the last is the sardius. This One, then, is the God of Abraham, Isaac, and Jacob.

   2. Round about the throne . . . twenty-four elders . . . Possibly twelve tribes and twelve apostles, but just as possibly purely figurative. White raiment and crowns (cf 3:5 and 21); these are "overcomers."

   3. OUT OF THE THRONE
Judgment . . . yet mercy (the rainbow). A throne of promise and restoration.

   4. Before the throne . . . Sea of glass (peaceful peoples, reflecting the Throne).

5. In the midst of the throne. Four living creatures, (not "beasts"). Symbolism interesting . . . but . . . four glorious creatures, majestic and beautiful, expressing some facet of the Revelation of God.
6. ACTION BEFORE THE THRONE. Vs. 8, the living creatures, elders . . . and then vs. 11, the son, "Worthy art thou."

II. THE MESSAGE OF THE PICTURE (Taken from the Song, etc.)
1. Briefly put, vitally important.
2. "Worthy art thou . . . for . . . for thy pleasure they were created."
3. Declaration of the full worthiness of God, must be accompanied by an attitude of humility on our part.

Conclusion: Have we fully learned the message of this song? Gaze on the picture in the background (quickly sketch) and join in the Hallelujah Chorus.

Appendix VII

Our second illustration of "Selective Method" (Selecting from a passage) is based on the sixteenth chapter of Acts.

Topic: "What Next?"

Introduction: The story of vss. 6-10.
  a. Vs. 6 . . . "Forbidden."
  b. Vs. 7 . . . Again, the same.
  c. Vs. 9 . . . The call.
  d. Vs. 10 . . . "He" saw . . . "We" went.

I. A SEEKER WAS WAITING. Vs. 14.
II. A TRAP WAS WAITING. Vs. 16.
III. A JAIL WAS WAITING. Vss. 19-24.

IV. A GLORIOUS WORK WAS WAITING. Vs. 30.

Conclusion: It matters not WHAT is next, so long as we follow the leadership of the Heavenly vision.

Appendix VIII

Our second illustration of the "Devotional Method" is a meditation based on Matthew 27:24-66, a Good Friday meditation.

Topic: "The Death of God"

Introduction: Familiar stories lose much of their detail in our minds. Surely, on Good Friday, we might well meditate on this story!

Vs. 24. Pilate pleads innocence.

Vs. 25. The Jews plead guilty.

Vss. 26-30. Ribald mockery, neither decent or just.

Vs. 31. Arrayed for death.

Vs. 32. Simon . . . compelled to bear the cross.

Vss. 33-34. "No opiates." Drained to the dregs . . .

Vs. 35. The crucifixion . . . No compulsion here. The gambling . . . no sign of extreme degradation . . . they treated Him just as another Jewish malefactor.

Vs. 36. Watching for . . .?

Vs. 37. The accusation (!)

Vs. 38. The company . . . two thieves.

Vss. 39-44. "If thou be . . . come down . . ." God refuses to take the Cross out of His program.

Vs. 45. Three hours of darkness.

Vss. 46-49. Forsaken . . .

Vs. 50. The Loud Cry . . . "It is finished."

Vss. 51-54. The response to all this . . . "Truly . . . the Son of God."

Vss. 55-57. The Women . . . (Always . . . the women stand by!)
Vss. 58-61. Burial, in a borrowed tomb.
Vss. 62-66. The seal and the guard.

Conclusion: Make sure no one gets fooled. These soldiers rendered great service in thus making sure. We believe, but for those who doubt, here is assurance.

And for now . . . here we leave Jesus . . . sealed in a borrowed tomb . . . but we must be conscious that He is there FOR US AND IN OUR STEAD.

Appendix IX

Our second illustration of the "Telescopic Method" has to do with the book of Jonah. This choice is made deliberately, for two reasons. Firstly, we have the utter dissimilarity between this book and John; and secondly, we can here illustrate this method in dealing with a disputed book. We take the first step, which is to read and re-read the book. In this case we discover that the book cannot be interpreted alone and apart from the rest of the Old Testament. Therefore a complete "background" study is imperative. We cannot explain the text without an understanding of how the text came to be and what its purpose was.

We conclude after careful investigation that the book of Jonah belongs to Jonah, the son of Amittai of Gath-hepher in Zebulon (II Kings 14:25). The time in which he prophesied was one of political revival in Israel. From a study of the thirteenth and fourteenth chapters of II Kings, we conclude that Jonah prophesied early in the reign of Jehoash. During the reign of Jehoahaz, the father of Jehoash, Syria constantly oppressed Israel. This God permitted, for reasons of his own. Then, under Jehoash, this oppression was overcome. In II Kings 14:25 Jonah is mentioned as having prophesied the recovery of Hamath. Now, if Jonah had been writing his prophecy at the time he is mentioned in II Kings, it seems likely that he would have mentioned the evil of the king who was so bad he was compared with "Jeroboam the son of Nebat," who seems to have been the epitome of evil in Israel. Therefore we conclude that it was either during or shortly after the suppression by Syria that the Israelites were objecting to Jonah bringing the message of God's mercy to Nineveh, or possibly some other non-Jewish nation or people. He may have been active in Israel at the time of Jeroboam the son of Jehoash, but the book was written, or sermon preached, before that time. We conclude that the book is a sermon, preached to reveal that God is the God of the Ninevites and other non-Jews, as well as of the Jews. The story of the fish is merely incidental, while 4:10-11 is the key, especially the inference that God has right to be concerned about many peoples on the basis of creation, much more than Jonah had a right to be concerned about the gourd.

All of this background study, revealing the prophecy as a sermon preached with a missionary purpose, may make our approach a restricted one, but we think not too much so. Perhaps this gives a fine chance to "teach" in the introduction, and to bring in a sort of "personal" touch (of Jonah) here and there as illustration.

Topic: "Shall We Honor Jonah?"

Introduction: Jonah was a man at first anti-missionary who, through difficult times and experiences came to have a missionary vision. (Story of Syrian oppression. Jewish hatred of all non-Jews . . . and Jonah's call to be a missionary. The objection by the people. Jonah preached this sermon to enforce the idea that God is a missionary God.) Shall we honor him?

I. SHALL WE HONOR A MAN WHO NEEDED THE PRESSURE OF A DISASTROUS STORM TO GET HIM STARTED RIGHT?

   1. The story of the fish merely incidental. It has clouded the main story.

   2. Arguments about the validity of the story futile. Jonah relates his experience.

   3. The most remarkable EVENT in the story is the storm with its immediate subsiding. The STORM turned Jonah about

to the right track . . . else he had not gone to Nineveh! (Maybe we would honor Jonah more if we were to recognize some of the upheavals of life in nature and otherwise as God-sent STORMS, and get onto the right track!)

II. SURELY WE OUGHT TO HONOR A MAN WHO WOULD NOT STOP SHORT OF SUCCESS!
(No half-way measures acceptable. Too often we fail just at this point.)

1. He delivered the WHOLE message of God, distasteful as it was to himself.

2. The whole city repented in sackcloth and ashes. Perhaps if we would deliver the WHOLE MESSAGE OF GOD, others might REPENT, and thus we would all honor the spirit of Jonah more.

III. PERHAPS WE DOUBT THE GIVING OF HONOR TO ONE WHO COULD NOT SEE GOD'S ALL-EMBRACING MERCY UNTIL A SCORCHING HEAT REMOVED HIS COMFORTING SHADE.

1. We must not forget the national pride of the Jew. (Religious pride, too.)

2. We must not forget that Jonah and his people had suffered for their religion, and under the very kind of people to whom he was now preaching.

3. Jonah capitulated to God's appeal (4:10-11) and recorded the story of his battle, even though shameful in parts, as a lesson to others.

Conclusion: ALL HONOR TO JONAH! He was frank enough to record his struggles, and as a result has left a great challenge to missionary zeal. We honor him not by words of praise, but by emulation. Doubtless if we could forget pride and creaturely comfort we would emulate him better.

Appendix X

For our second illustration of the "Selective Method" (Selecting from the entire Bible) we study the word "Rod." Our primary preparation is the same as that for the former sermon: collation, selection, exegesis, reading, meditation, and a resultant outline. This is a much more simple study because of the scarcity of reference to Rods, and the readiness with which these references fall into logical sermonic order. The resultant outline, then,

Topic: "Rods of God"

Introduction: Refer to Prov. 10:13 "In the lips of him that hath understanding, wisdom is found; but a rod is for the back of him that is without understanding." And Prov. 29:15, "The rod and reproof give wisdom; but a child left to himself bringeth his mother to shame." And vs. 17, "Correct thy son and he shall give thee rest; yea, he shall give delight to thy soul."

These thoughts direct our minds to the proverb, "Spare the rod and spoil the child," and this reminds us of Hebrews 12:6, "Whom the Lord loveth he chasteneth." And this reminds us of Revelation 2:27, "And he shall rule them with a rod of iron."

BUT . . . GOD HAS OTHER RODS.

I. THE ROD THAT IS A SYMBOL OF DIVINE AUTHORITY.
   Ex. 4:20, "And Moses took the rod of God in his hands"; and Num. 17:8, "The rod of Aaron was budded."
   1. Moses and Aaron had to learn to bow to authority.
   2. Only at great cost did the Israelites learn this lesson, and then they seemed to forget too easily.
   3. The note of authority and the recognition of authority are sadly lacking today.

II. THE ROD THAT IS A SYMBOL OF DIVINE COMFORT.
   Ps. 23:4, "Thy rod and thy staff they comfort me."
   1. This rod is a symbol of the shepherd-heart of God.

2. As the sheep becomes really identified with the flock he learns not to fear this rod, but to seek its comfort and help.
   3. Comfort is lacking today. We are not following close to the shepherd.

III. THE ROD THAT IS A SYMBOL OF DIVINE REDEMPTION.
   Isa. 11:1, "And there shall come forth a rod." and Ps. 74:2, "The rod of thine inheritance which thou hast redeemed."
   1. The rod as a fact. An instrument in the hands of God for reaching His sheep.
   2. There is an affinity between the Redeemer and the redeemed.
   3. The "Redemption" of thine "Inheritance." ! ! ! Useless cost!

Conclusion: As we profit by these Rods of God we save ourselves the Rod of divine rebuke. (Perhaps one might well conclude with the teaching of Rev. 2:27 — translating it carefully into "shepherd them with a staff of iron" — referring not to any brutal harshness but to a kindness and concern which is nevertheless inexorable in its demands.)

Appendix XI

Our second illustration of "Preaching from History" is based on the history of Israel from a theocracy to a monarchy and then to dissolution as a nation. Our method follows the former procedure. We first carefully read the story, which covers from Judges 21:25 to Second Chronicles 36:20. Having read and re-read the story, having eliminated in what seems almost a brutal fashion, we glean the following material:

Judges 21:25 reads, "In those days there was no king in Israel; every man did that which was right in his own eyes." Then in I Samuel 8 we find that Samuel was growing old. His sons were judges, because they were priests, but "They walked not in his ways, but turned aside after lucre, and took bribes, and perverted judgment." Then the elders came to Samuel and said, "Behold, thou art old, and thy sons walk not in thy ways; now make us a king to judge us like all the nations." Samuel disliked the idea and prayed earnestly. God answered, "Hearken unto the voice of all the people in all that they say unto thee: for they have not rejected thee, but they have rejected me, that I should not reign over them." Then were issued certain warnings and the people answered Samuel, "Nay, but we will have a king over us, that we also may be like the nations, and that our king may judge us, and go out before us, and fight our battles." Verse 22 reads. "And the Lord said to Samuel, Hearken unto their voice, and make them a king." (This reminds us very much of Psalms 106:15, "And he gave them their request, but sent leanness unto their souls.") Saul is anointed king. Wars and conflicts are reported. David was a good man, a man after God's own heart, but he committed a great sin. Solomon was wise, but moral deterioration was evident, most clearly in that while he built a beautiful temple, he raised weak sons. He may have been wise, but unwisely chose Jeroboam the son of Nebat as a ruler and leader. The prophet Ahijah told Jeroboam that he was to rule over ten tribes, and God promised him blessing if he would walk in the godly way. Solomon died and Rehoboam reigned. Rehoboam was questioned, as reported in 1 Kings 12, and sought counsel of both old and young. He forsook the counsel of the wise elders and followed that of the hot-headed youths. Rebellion followed and Jeroboam was made king over the ten tribes, in fulfillment of the prophecy of Ahijah. Rehoboam kept only Judah and Benjamin. This is a far cry from the days of Samuel! The history of the two portions of the kingdom are tragically similar. King after king follows in the steps of Rehoboam and Jeroboam. Soon Israel was scattered, and Judah was kept but only for the purpose of the later fulfillment of prophecy. Israel ceased, as a nation. She ceased potentially when she asked for a king . . . "To be like other nations." We cannot but suggest to the student in this connection that he read the words found in Isaiah, in the 48th chapter, 17-22, and in the 49th chapter, the first six verses. The story would be spiritually incomplete without these references!

Now again we eliminate and rearrange and exegete and meditate. Ultimately the following outline is brought out, based on the whole message of the fascinating story, fascinating in spite of its tragic ending.

Topic: "A Monarchy that Failed"

Introduction: Reading the history of Israel may seem to be a dry matter. There is not an easy style, and there is much monotonous repetition. Yet in this story God has preserved and revealed great spiritual truths. (Here we would insert a quickly painted picture of Israel as conquerors of Canaan . . . as under the Judges . . . as a nation, and then, as dispersed and scattered.) The conditions that obtained at the time of the Judges, and even at Judges 21:25 could have been all to the good had not the theocratic conception died first. (I Samuel 8:7, "They have not rejected thee, they have rejected me.")

I. THE REPLACING OF A THEOCRACY, CONTAINING ALL THE NECESSARY ELEMENTS OF SUCCESS WITH A MONARCHY, CONTAINING ALL THE ELEMENTS OF FAILURE, WAS CAUSED BY A WRONG PERSPECTIVE.
   1. "That we may be like other nations." Looked OUT and not UP. I Sam. 8:20-21.
   2. Same vss. "That he (king) may go before us, . . ." They looked to a man, and forgot their sure hope, God.
   3. The foundation rift was caused by a failure of spiritual perspective.
      a. Samuel's sons were ungodly, yet priests.
      b. "They have rejected me." I Sam. 8:9.

II. THE CAUSE OF THE BREAK-UP OF THE MONARCHY, EVEN WHEN THE GRACE OF GOD WAS AVAILABLE TO GUIDE IT TO SUCCESS, WAS, AGAIN, WRONG PERSPECTIVE.
   1. Saul looked out to doubtful conquest, instead of up to sure victory.
   2. David looked down into his neighbor's garden when he should have been looking up from the Garden of Prayer.

3. Solomon looked to mental wisdom, but overlooked moral deterioration. (He built a beautiful temple, but forgot to rear beautiful sons.)

4. Rehoboam looked to hot-headed youth instead of level-headed age.

5. The succeeding kings of the divided kingdom followed mostly in the steps of Rehoboam and Jeroboam (instead of where God wanted to lead them) . . . unto the dissolution of their respective nations.

III. THE ELEMENT NECESSARY FOR REPLACING THE THEOCRACY AFTER THE FALL OF THIS MONARCHY IS . . . RIGHT PERSPECTIVE. (Based on Isaiah 48:12-22 and 49:1-6).

1. God regrets the outcome of Israel's wrong perspective. (48:18)

2. He sets before Israel the right perspective. (48:20)

3. He holds this light out to all the world. (49:6)

Conclusion: What is our perspective? Look down and die . . . look up and live. Look to God, and victory is sure.

Appendix XII

Our second illustration of "Homiletically Interpreting Events" considers Pentecost. Pentecost is surely an outstanding event in the history of the Christian church. Too often we preach concerning the experience of Pentecost as though it were mere history and had no practical value to us. Some, on the other hand, have merely sought to copy the apostolic experience given at Pentecost without understanding the full meaning of that event. After careful study, as suggested in the main chapter dealing with this method, we might well develop the following as an outline:

Topic: "The Power of Pentecost"

Introduction: Dwell on the current misunderstanding, and also refer to the historic establishment of the feast and important implications in it.

I. (Cf. Rom. 8:23) THE HOLY SPIRIT AT PENTECOST WAS THE FIRST-FRUITS OF GOD'S GRACE, EVEN AS THE FIRST FRUITS OF MAN'S LABOR.
   1. The gift is by grace (else not "gift").
   2. The gift was appropriate.
   3. The gift both sealed the past and assured the future.

II. (Cf. Ex. 12 and 19) AT PENTECOST THE LAW WAS GIVEN, AND ALSO (ACTS 2) THE HOLY SPIRIT.
   1. The law at Pentecost sealed the covenant of grace in the Passover. (The Lamb!)
   2. The Spirit at Pentecost sealed the covenant of grace in the Atonement. (The Lamb!)

III. THE SUPREME AND LASTING BLESSING OF PENTECOST IS NOT IN MERE HISTORIC FACTS.
   1. Offer first fruits? Good.
   2. Live by Spirit vs Law? Good.
   3. Supreme importance — "Power after." Result: Witnesses.

Conclusion: Ours is not to repeat apostolic experience but to obey apostolic precept. It may be that power in witnessing will be granted to us at Pentecost.

Appendix XIII

For our second illustration of the "Biographical Method" we study a character generally well known yet much misunderstood, Thomas. Thomas has suffered much at the hands of those who should have been more sympathetic in their treatment. We do not have much information given to us, but we will find enough once we diligently look into the record. Our procedure is the same as that for Mark. Finally we produce the following outline.

Topic: "The Tenacious Twin"

Introduction: Thomas fairly well known, usually misunderstood. Called "Doubting Thomas," and there left. We call him "The Tenacious Twin" both to be different and to be more nearly correct at the last. That he doubted is true . . . but . . .

I. THE MAN HIMSELF.
   1. Family.
      a. No proof.
      b. Thomas not his NAME. Comes from Thoma, Hebrew, or Didymas Greek, both transliterated into Thomas and Didymas.
      c. Cf. Matt. 13:55 and Mark 6:3: Judas a brother of Jesus. (Ancient tradition says this Judas was called Thomas or Didymas, by the disciples even though his twin brother had died, utterly to separate him from Judas Iscariot on the one hand and Judas Simon's son on the other. Some identify him with the writer of "Jude." No proof for either of these, but the suggestion is interesting.)
   2. His Call and Ordination.
      Call not stated. In Matt. 10:3, sent out with "Matthew the Publican," on the trip "Two by two." Heard that great ordination sermon.

II. THE CHARACTER OF THE MAN (Revealed mostly in John's Gospel). (Somewhere one wrote, "In Thomas we have a man incredulous but tenacious; despondent but true; with little hope but much courage; sincere in love though perplexed in faith; neither running to the right conclusion as Peter might have done, nor rushing from it into danger and dishonor as Peter did.")
   1. "Let us also go that we may die with him." Pessimistic, but loyal and courageous. John 11:16,

2. "Lord, we know not whither thou goest, and how can we know the way?" Doubting, seeing all difficulties, yet desirous to KNOW. John 14:5.

3. "Except I see . . . and touch . . . I will not believe." John 20:24-27.

Incredulous, demands proof, but . . . note . . . is susceptible to that when offered! (There are none so blind as they that will not see.)

III. HIS MESSAGE TO US.

The greatest confession in the New Testament, comparable only to that of Peter at Caeserea Philippi . . . "My Lord and My God!"

Conclusion:

1. Thomas is our greatest proof that the disciples were not mislead by self-hypnosis, or any similar hypothetical attitude.

2. Thomas our greatest example of constant devotion when facing sure disaster. (The martyrs knew the risen Lord. Thomas at this time did not.)

3. Thomas believed because the fact which was too good to hope for became too certain to reject.

Appeal: John 20:29, "Thomas, because thou hast seen me, thou hast believed; blessed are they that have not seen, and yet they have believed."

Here Jesus challenges us to a great faith, and promises an adequate reward.

Appendix XIV

Our second illustration of "Sermons from Biographies Plus" deals with the contact of Jesus with the Nobleman. The lesson is found in John 4:46-54.

Topic: "The Nameless Nobleman"

For our introduction we present this nameless man. The question, "Why is this man included in John's manuscript? Answer, "A sign." Of what? God's power working through Jesus.

I. THE MAN.

1. King's office . . . stern, brave, taciturn, keen-minded, alert, practical, (not at all mystical), rich.

2. A father.
    a. Profound affection for his son.
       Had heard of Jesus. Travelled 15 or 20 miles for him (Capernaum to Cana). Love inspired this venture.
    b. Last chance . . . desperate . . . son dying.

3. No quibbler.
   Was not looking for argument. Wanted to get right down to business. "Never mind talking about your signs. My son is dying. Come down."

4. Man of reason and faith.
    a. Faith in the last analysis is reasonable.
    b. Keen mind recognizes the note of authority in another.
    c. He believed the WORD of Jesus, and WENT HOME ON ITS STRENGTH.

5. A whole-hearted man.
    a. He investigated the hour of recovery (7th hour). Left nothing to chance.
    b. He and his whole house were converted.

II. THE METHOD.

1. Satire. "Except ye see signs."
   Jesus knew all men. He knew this man was not after the healing as a sign, but as a means to retaining his boy who was dying. Yet He uses satire, possibly to awaken the man, to draw him out.

2. Severity. "Go thy way, thy son liveth." A severe test of faith and obedience.
3. The sign given. Jesus led the man beyond the ordinary realms of life, and gave a sign.

III. THE MESSAGE TO US.
1. Christ knows the deepest in all men.
2. His challenges to faith are reasonable.
3. The exercise of faith is prerequisite to the experience of faith. Let us give our nobleman a name. He surely is a man of faith, or "Faithful."

Appeal on III, 3: "Take action." If you will, in faith then shall appear to you the evidence of this sign, that God surely works through Jesus Christ.

Appendix XV

For our second illustration of "Sermons from Geography" we present the outline resultant upon our study of Bethany. The homiletic development of this outline is quite different from the outline in the sermon on Kadesh Barnea. The study of geography is the same for both sermons. In this one we take the major portion of the sermon time in what is rightly called introduction. It is our desire so to portray the actions which once took place around Bethany, in impressionistic story form, that when we present the major divisions of our sermon each division will be so near to the other that the "attack" will be greatly strengthened.

Our sermon topic is "The Transciency of Glory." The Scripture lesson is Luke 24:13-53.

Introduction: Bethany, a little village, two miles S. E. of Jerusalem, across the Kidron, at the foot of the Mount of Olives, on the road between Jericho and Jerusalem, just where that road begins its steep descent into the Valley of Jehosaphat. Scarcity of mention, but intimacy of interest.

In imagination go over to Bethany. We find a dilapidated, wretched, poverty-stricken village, El Lazari by name, of 30 or 40 small houses. Here the house and tomb of Lazarus are shown us, but both are probably fictitious. Across the vally we see the minarets and towers of Jerusalem . . . and our minds jump back nineteen centuries, to the time of Christ. A young man appears, and tells his story.

> Here tradesmen and tribesmen, religious pilgrims and military cavalcades often passed by (to and from Jericho).
>
> Jesus often went through alone and with disciples.
>
> Here was the home of Lazarus . . . , etc.
>
> Here lived Simon the Leper, and the grateful woman.
>
> Jesus often lodged within the village. He often retired here after strenuous days in Jerusalem, especially in that last week. From here Jesus started that journey on the Day of Entry.
>
> From here Jesus ascended.

The youth disappears. The vision fades . . . stark wretchedness on every hand, in contrast with the glory of the vision, prompts the query . . . WHY? With such a glorious past . . . why this wretched present? Where is the gratitude of Mary and Martha and Lazarus? Where the love of that woman who anointed Him? Where the hospitality of the home of Simon? Where the vision of "Him that cometh in the name of the Lord?" Where the thrill of the message . . . "Ye men of Galilee, why stand ye gazing? This same Jesus . . . shall come . . . in like manner as ye have seen Him go." WHY . . . ?

I. A GLORIOUS HISTORY NO GUARANTEE OF A GLORIOUS FUTURE. (Let nations beware!)

II. GLORIOUS EXPERIENCES OF DIVINE POWER NO GUARANTEE OF CONTINUANCE OF THE DIVINE PRESENCE.

III. GLORIOUS VISIONS OF ETERNAL MAJESTY NO GUARANTEE OF HUMAN VISIONS OF TEMPORAL RESPONSIBILITY.

Conclusion: By all means let us glory in a glorious past, and rejoice in happy visions. Let us be warned by the history of Bethany that we be faithful, lest we too fall into disrepair and disrepute.

Appendix XVI

For our second illustration of dealing with the Parables we turn to Luke 10:25-37, the parable of the Samaritan. Our background study and purpose is the same as that for the first sermon, and finally we produce the following outline.

Topic: "The Waterloo of Law"

Introduction: Vss. 25-29 reveal the occasion for the parable. Lawyer — stood up and tempted (tested) him (tested Christ's attitude toward the law ... sought Christ's attitude toward the common idea of the works of the law). The emphasis was on the "Do." Christ makes the lawyer answer himself. (Christ always upheld the law, but not the Pharisaical interpretation of it.) Then, vs. 29, the lawyer feels that he has been "shown up." He tries to make it appear that all along he has been leading up to this next question, and trying to snare Jesus on this problem. Then comes the parable ... to answer the query as to "How does the law work out?"

I. THE FIGURES USED.
  1. Man, likely a Jew ... (from Jerusalem to Jericho).
  2. The road ... robber-infested.
  3. The priest, representative of religious law.
  4. The Levite, representative of ceremonial law.
  5. The Samaritan, representative of the point of the parable. (The law of love, cf. vs. 27a, Love!)

II. THE PURPOSE OF THE PARABLE.
  1. To answer the false premise in the lawyer's question. The problem is not "find a neighbor," but "be a neighbor."

2. To reveal the failure of the law. Philanthropy is not a road to glory . . . but love to God must eventuate in love to man. (Law says do this and live; grace says live and do this.)

   a. The priest passed by . . . not heartlessly, but because else, touching blood, he would be ceremoniously unclean. Religious law binds one's hands.

   b. The Levite passes by . . . not heartlessly, but because otherwise he too would be ceremonially unclean. Again, the law tied his hands. Study a comparison of law and grace.*

(1) Law...given by Moses	Grace and truth by Jesus Christ
(2) Law...written on stone	Grace...on the hearts
(3) Law...(letter) killeth	Grace...entrance of thy words...life
(4) Law...glory fadeth	Grace...glory excelleth
(5) Law...with veiled face	Grace...an unveiled face
(6) Law...given on Mt. Sinai	Grace...on Mt. Calvary
(7) Law...emphasis on works	Grace...emphasis on faith
(8) Law...life by doing	Grace...life by believing
(9) Law...brings a curse	Grace...brings blessing
(10) Law...commands	Grace...enables
(11) Law...no excuse	Grace...supplies the Advocate
(12) Law...no pardon	Grace...reconciles and atones
(13) Law...reveals sin	Grace...reveals God
(14) Law...condemns	Grace...redeems
(15) Law...IS FETTERED	GRACE IS FREE TO ACT IN LOVE

   c. The Samaritan, morally no better than the priest and the Levite, but unfettered by laws, is able to do that which is needed.

III. THE APPLICATION OF THE PARABLE.

Live by grace and not by the nice observance of the law. Go and be a neighbor. Quibbling over the law is to no avail.

---

* Dr. G. C. Morgan's class lectures.

Appendixes 155

Appendix XVII

We present herewith our second illustration of "Preaching from Prayers." As we have already warned this was chosen for its difficulty. We are convinced that it will reveal great value in this approach. Passage, Genesis 4:1-15.

Topic: "Three Prayers"

Introduction: What is prayer? The soul, reaching out to God. Petition may be present, or only implied, or entirely absent. Does God hear and answer prayers? And what is the result of prayer?

I. THE CHARACTERS WHO PRAYED . . . CAIN AND ABEL.
  1. Cain. May have been looked on as fulfillment of Gen. 3:15 . . . name, possibly "The established one" . . . root of word suggests spear, transfixed, quivering.
     a. Haughty, favored, proud, selfish.
     b. Quick-tempered, especially if brother out-does him.
     c. See vs. 7, "Unto thee is its desire, but thou shouldest rule over it."
  2. Abel. Name . . . "Nothingness" . . . may refer to "disappointed hope."
     Humble, patient, kind, retiring . . . yet an inner consecration to service. . . .

II. THE CONDITIONS THAT SURROUNDED THE PRAYERS.
  1. No ceremonial laws (so far as we know).
  2. General recognition of God as above all, etc.
  3. The immediate surrounding.
     a. Abel offered the "Firstlings of his flock."
     b. Cain offered "Of the fruit of the ground."
     c. God's fire kindled Abel's offering.
     d. Satan's flame kindled Cain's soul.

e. Cain invited Abel to walk in the field, and "Hacked him to pieces." Brutal, premeditated murder.

f. Cain, accused, curses . . . is not penitent but rather bowed down with a sense of the burden of his own punishment.

III. THE ELEMENTS OF THESE THREE PRAYERS.
   1. Abel . . . Thanksgiving and Worship.
   2. Cain . . . Self-justification.
   3. Cain . . . "Cry-baby."

IV. THE RESULTS OF THESE PRAYERS.
   1. Abel's . . . accepted by God but roused jealousy in the soul of a sinner.
   2. Cain's . . . rejected by God and roused his own anger.
   3. Cain's . . . brought a curse, but held that curse in leash. Vs. 15.

Conclusion. Lessons for us.

1. Haughty prayers valueless, even harmful.

2. If the prayer is valueless, fault is in self . . . not God, or others.

3. We must rule over the sin that ruins the offering.

4. Appeal . . . cf. vs. 4:10 and Heb. 12:24 . . . "The blood of sprinkling" speaks better things than Abel's. His cried for vengeance . . . Jesus' called for pardon. Sincere humble prayer makes this available to us.

Appendix XVIII

Our second study in "Preaching from the Psalms" is based on the nineteenth Psalm. We entitle it:

Topic: "An Improvement on Natural Theology"

I. NATURE WITNESSES TO GOD AND HIS GLORY. Vss. 1-6.
   1. The heavens. Vs. 1
   2. The firmament. Vss. 2-3 (The passing "times"?)
   3. The earth. Vs. 4a
   4. The sun. Vs. 4b (Constant and penetrating)

II. IMPROVEMENT ON THE WITNESS WHICH NATURE GIVES. Vss. 7-11
   1. Law . . . perfect . . . restores the soul.
   2. Testimony . . . sure . . . makes wise the simple.
   3. Precepts . . . right . . . rejoicing the heart.
   4. Commandments . . . pure . . . enlightening the eyes.
   5. Fear . . . clean . . . enduring forever.
   6. Ordinances . . . true and righteous altogether . . . by them is thy servant warned.

Conclusion: Need for earnest concern. 12-13. Confident benediction. Vs. 14.

We should note that there are in vss 7-11 six words which are synonymous to Torah, each with an adjectival predicate and a participle relating the law of Jehovah to the individual experience. Each synonym has its own particular shade of meaning, revealing the genuine value of the study of Hebrew for such work as this. Only out of an intimate knowledge of Hebrew can the expositor get the greatest possible value from the Psalms and give this value to his people.

Date Due

Fri m	1:00	NO 03 '04	
SEP 2	10:30		
SEP 28	2:15		
Oct 15	2:00		
STRICT RESERVE	FEB 10		
4:00	DEC 23 '82		
12:00	JAN 5 '83		
11:00	Jan. 24		
1/2 8:30			
10:00			
8:30 1/2			
MAY 21			
10:35			
12:35			
1:30			
2:30			
4:00			
8:30 12/10			

PRINTED IN U.S.A.